Lawrence Lam provides a clear fra[mework] management teams by highlighting the .... founders successful. *The Founder Effect* is a must-read for anyone looking to understand what sets top leadership apart.

— Chip Wilson,
Founder of Lululemon

The Founder Effect breaks away from conventional business theory, offering a deep dive into the out-of-the-box entrepreneurial mindset. It explores the innovative strategies that have been key to Chemist Warehouse's enduring success and growth.

— Jack Gance,
Chairman and Co-Founder, Chemist Warehouse

The Founder Effect isn't just another business book. It's a powerhouse of insight that unveils the secrets to how we operate— capturing the essence of a founder's mindset and how we have forged success and growth at Flight Centre.

— Graham Turner, Global Managing Director, CEO, and
Co-Founder, Flight Centre Travel Group

Providing essential insights for evaluating executive management teams, Lawrence Lam's *The Founder Effect* is an indispensable resource for achieving long-term and sustainable success.

— Robert Millner AO,
Chairman and Non-Executive Director, Soul Patts

The Founder Effect offers crucial insights for executives and management teams striving for long-term success. Lawrence Lam provides a clear framework for evaluating leadership and driving sustainable growth, which is key for any forward-thinking organisation.

— Chris Davies,
CEO, Telstra Superannuation

THE
FOUNDER
EFFECT

THE
FOUNDER
EFFECT

Three Pillars of Success in Founder-Led Companies

LAWRENCE LAM

WILEY

First published 2025 by John Wiley & Sons Australia, Ltd

ISBN: 978-1-394-29371-1

A catalogue record for this book is available from the National Library of Australia

Registered Office
John Wiley & Sons Australia, Ltd. Level 4, 600 Bourke Street, Melbourne, VIC 3000, Australia

For details of our global editorial offices, customer services, and more information about Wiley products visit us at www.wiley.com.

Wiley also publishes its books in a variety of electronic formats and by print-on-demand. Some content that appears in standard print versions of this book may not be available in other formats.

Cover and part opener image: © DV Imaginarium/Adobe Stock
Cover design by Wiley

Internal permissions: Figure P1-01 © Archive PL/Alamy Stock Photo; Figure 5-1 © Solaris/ Alamy Stock Photo

Set in ITC Cheltenham Std 10.5/16pt by Straive, Chennai, India

SKY80FCC0FD-26D3-4078-97DA-592704364AAF_011525

To the one who is always by my side on this shinkansen,
and to the one peacefully dreaming as I pen these words,
I love you both.

Contents

About the author

Lawrence Lam is an investor, founder, and author with over two decades of experience in global financial markets, dedicated to uncovering what truly drives long-term success in business. As founder of Lumenary Investment Management, Lawrence draws on years of analysing, researching, and interviewing global executive teams to identify the traits that set exceptional companies apart. *The Founder Effect* distils these insights into a practical framework for evaluating leadership and governance—tailored for investors, executives and board directors alike.

Beyond his work in investments, Lawrence is deeply committed to civic initiatives that support businesses and promote family-friendly urban spaces. On weekends, you'll find him with his young family exploring the many cafes and shops of Melbourne, and on the basketball court; an avid player since age eight, Lawrence refuses to retire from competitive basketball despite multiple surgeries— because, as he puts it, 'ball is life'.

Learn more at lawrencelam.org.

Keep in touch

Get updates about Lawrence's founder-led companies fund and discover new founder-led companies each quarter.

Introduction

'In the company of sages, there is constant delight.'
— **Lao Tzu**

Human nature compels us to present ourselves and our tribe in the best possible light to the outside world. The corporate world is no different. Management teams foster an image to highlight their strengths and opportunities, while downplaying the challenges and dysfunctions within. *You don't air your dirty laundry.* There are strong incentives to craft the perfect image to reassure employees, investors, board directors, and customers. This is expected and understood as part of the corporate game. However, when discerning investors, board directors, and other executives peer into the inner workings of a company from the outside, the curated image portrayed by internal managers offers little real value—instead, what is of value is gaining a realistic insight into the potential of the leadership team, the motivations of the people in the team, and their ability to grow the business. It is only once the façade is removed that a true understanding of how a company *thinks* is revealed. After all, a company is a mere collection of decisions made over time that, once accumulated over many years, steer the company in a certain direction. Once you can understand how well a company thinks, you will be able to realistically judge for yourself its potential for success.

This book is not intended to be another general leadership skills manual. Rather, it aims to provide a framework for assessing the effectiveness of management teams from the perspective of readers wearing several different hats: executive, board director, investor. At the core of this book is a framework for the assessment of the *people* in management teams.

This book takes the perspective of an outsider looking into a company. While outsiders may not have the benefit of insider knowledge, they can resourcefully utilise all the publicly available tools investors have at their disposal. In such a data-rich era, every investor has in their arsenal the ability to assess, to a reasonable level of accuracy, the strengths and weaknesses of a management team. Using the Framework in this book, I show you how to make such assessments by sharing my experiences of interviewing, researching, and analysing the temperament and effectiveness of management teams that enable them to make sound commercial judgements. Every company and sector is different but, as you will see, the principles of human nature and teamwork are largely universal. Although it may appear that the assessment of management teams is entirely subjective, there are objective indicators which allow an outsider to form a view of a team's capabilities.

For executives who will use this book as an internal assessment and benchmarking tool, the ability to view one's own team from the perspective of an outsider will serve as a realistic appraisal of your team's strengths and weaknesses. It will inform you of how you are perceived by the outside world—savvy investors and customers can see through the public relations spin, therefore informing you of the necessary adaptations needed to genuinely improve your management capabilities and chemistry.

Board directors should take a keen interest in this area as the stewards of shareholder capital. It is crucial that they make unbiased and independent assessments of their management teams as they are the ones that have empowered managers with executing the vision and strategy of the company—and yet we so often see management teams exerting significant influence when it comes to assessing their own performance. *If you ask a chef how their dish was supposed to taste, they will always tell you any imperfections were meant to be.* Instead of relying on management reports to form a view, board directors should start with an independent view, but evolve that assessment by adapting to new inputs from management reporting, employee feedback, customer sentiment, and market perception, all of which dynamically shift over time. By doing so, board directors can elevate their governance of executive teams, strategically incentivise them, and proactively address potential personnel challenges by shaping an effective decision-making framework within the organisation.

Why I wrote this book

Let me share how I became inspired to put pen to paper and write a book about what it takes to create and recognise great management teams—more specifically, how I came to believe in the unique effect of founders on how their businesses are managed and run. Over my 20-odd years in financial services, I have seen a plethora of ways companies have been run. Through my various roles—which started with the Australian federal financial services regulator the Australian Prudential Regulation Authority (APRA), followed by a corporate advisory role at Deloitte, investment banking roles at Royal Bank of Scotland and MUFG, my position as a professional investor in the investment firm I founded, Lumenary Investment Management, and as a consultant to boards—I came across a multitude of executives who I would deem highly intelligent and motivated. However, the majority of those people could not create long-lasting success in the companies they were leading. Sure, they could create value over a few years—but not decades. Only a rare few could sustain success over the long haul.

It is often said that the earliest phase of a career is the most influential in shaping our perspective. This is because the observations we make when our minds are most open are often the least clouded by cognitive biases. Paradoxically, it is the lack of experience that allows us to see things with a certain clarity, free from preconceptions. For me, the first time I encountered a group of truly exceptional company leaders was early in my corporate advisory career, as I worked across various industries and companies (more on this in the next section). After that initial encounter, I became keenly attuned to the inner workings of companies and their leaders over the following decades. While most management teams I encountered fit the mould of the status quo, every now and then, I would meet executives who stood out—demonstrating the very traits I had noticed earlier in my career. What set these exceptional leaders apart was not their experience, qualifications, or skills, but an intangible mindset—a set of behavioural characteristics that did not show up on paper but were reflected in the way they ran their companies. These traits became a recurring theme in the successful companies I observed, leading me to view them not as an output of brilliant companies, but as a precursor of long-term corporate success. This realisation inspired me to develop a framework for identifying these traits, helping to predict which companies would flourish. By sharing these insights, I hope to help the corporate community recognise and celebrate these quiet achievers for their consistent excellence and unconventional leadership.

Now, let me share with you the story of my first discovery—how one particular company caught my attention and became my first case study in understanding the foundations of true, sustained success.

My first discovery

One of my first roles involved advising corporations on their hedging strategies, risk management policies, and use of derivatives. These were the heady days prior to the Global Financial Crisis (GFC), which meant all sorts of interesting and creative risk management instruments were being employed by corporates to avoid the ultimate sin at the time: a 'lazy balance sheet'. To eke out every bit of return, it would be common practice to maximise borrowings and invest in complex financial instruments, or to shift assets off the balance sheet using special purpose vehicles (SPVs). To keep up with the competition, corporates were encouraged by their advisors to pursue these aggressive strategies and fall in line with market best practice—and who wouldn't want to adopt best practice? It was this herd mentality (which in hindsight was entrenched by the preceding decade of growing prosperity) that led to a nonchalant attitude and a lack of questioning of the commonly accepted approaches at the time. However, as a fresh-eyed observer in the early phase of my career, I had the benefit of little experience. My role was focused on analysing and devising recommendations to businesses on their optimal use of financial capital. This required an understanding of the financial statements — being able to see how a company could optimise its capital structure to shore up its financial strength, or raise funding to accelerate growth through debt and hedge against market risk with derivative instruments. The benefit of such a role was the exposure to all types of businesses. No matter what size or sector they belong to, all businesses have financial statements. And these financials reveal a company's underlying health just like a blood test indicates the health of a person. But more than that, these numbers reveal intention — they show where decision-makers are prioritising their capital. I was able to answer questions about their business using these numbers. Were they a risk-averse organisation looking to hedge every dollar of exposure? Were they in growth phase and looking to raise funds by issuing financial instruments to fuel their growth projects? The numbers provided me with a window into the inner thought processes of a plethora of businesses that spanned a wide variety of industries. What I saw was the majority of companies behaving relatively similarly — their levels of debt would broadly be in line; the types of risk management tools to hedge against interest rate and foreign exchange rates were the same, or thereabouts; the types of projects they would pursue had a similar payback period (which was unsurprising, as they were all advised by the same banks). But one day my perception changed when I was assigned to work on behalf of a local wine manufacturing business.

What caught my attention at first was its growth. Here was a winemaker based in rural Australia that was consistently increasing revenues over its 40-year history. Moreover, it was a sensibly run company, with minimal debt and steady margins. It also held more cash than other typical companies I had seen. As I delved deeper, I discovered the company was not listed. It was still privately held by the founding family and was now being managed by the second generation of the family, who had developed a subsidiary wine brand designed for the overseas market — which turned out to be a huge success in the US and

China; a key driver of its recent growth. And as the numbers showed, the business needed very little external capital. Instead, it reinvested profits back into such growth projects.

This 40-year-old winemaker did the opposite of what was trending. While most companies at the time relied heavily on bank funding and avoided a large cash balance in the pursuit of growth, this company, bearing the weight of its founding family's legacy in both its name and logo, was interested in the organic, longer-term growth of the brand. Over time, as I had the opportunity to hear and understand the management team's approach, I began to appreciate the long-term nature of their actions. As a steward of the company, the CEO and son of the founder was driven to create a long-lasting company that would continue to bear fruit for his children and grandchildren. The business strategy was centred around longevity and delivering sustainable growth. Instead of borrowing heavily to fund growth projects, the business preferred to keep a large cash buffer and instead reinvest the income to organically grow, thereby avoiding the influence of external financiers and remaining in control of its own destiny.

As you might expect, having the family name inscribed in the company brand instils a deep sense of pride, but more importantly, a level of responsibility to safeguard its reputation for future generations. The company was committed to protecting this legacy at all costs, often choosing to launch new subsidiary brands for international markets to avoid any confusion with its established domestic identity. Decisions on new ventures were approached with a long-term perspective, measured over decades, rather than the usual three-to-five-year horizon common in most corporations. This approach also explained why the company was so cautious with the use of external capital — its financial foundations were to be strengthened over time, not diluted with lenders and more shareholders. This allowed the company to acquire competitors during industry downturns, as it remained financially strong when others had over-leveraged. The sustained success this winemaker achieved and the style of business it ran attracted me. I began to seek out more companies like this to observe. But as I was to learn in the next phase of my career, such companies were quite rare.

Every now and then I would encounter a company with a similar philosophy but, unless I sought them out deliberately, it was very unlikely one would come across my desk fortuitously. By then I knew the characteristics of these founder-led companies and I could find them in the public markets. What I realised was that I could learn just as much from these founder-led companies as from their counterparts — the non-founder-led companies, where the bureaucratic disease had taken hold and a myopic quarterly focus had become entrenched.

There was no better way to contrast these opposing styles than by comparing them with the very organisations I worked for. Instead of a long-term focus on brand building and generating sustainable revenue streams, the multinational investment banks I represented were tied down by their own bureaucratic processes and internal infighting, which handcuffed their ability to adapt quickly to market needs. Instead of a company motivated and aligned with its shareholders, I observed investment bankers engaged in lobbying to secure the highest possible annual bonus they could by redesigning key performance indicators (KPIs) and shifting their targets with clever, well-reasoned presentations. It was an annual dance that would occur in the months leading up to bonus season. So ingrained was this culture of the annual bonus that executive management teams were themselves part of this annual dance.

The value of an investment banker to the global management team was measured by their ability to meet short-term targets — typically set within a three-to-five-year timeframe, with progress reviewed annually. The frequent turnover of staff eroded any sense of loyalty or commitment to the business's long-term growth. Instead of functioning as a cohesive team, we became more like mercenaries, assembled to complete the next task, and nothing more. Our attention was squarely focused on personal bonuses, and the game became a test of our ability to demonstrate individual contributions to the annual budget targets. What makes the experience of an investment bank interesting is that the sheer brainpower within the team was undisputable. The capability and work ethic were not in contention. But in comparison to the founder-led companies I had observed earlier in my career, our motivations were not aligned with the long-term interests of our shareholders. Because of the way the incentives were structured and the culture within investment banking, the focus of decision-making worked only on short time horizons. There was no sense of delayed gratification — almost everything we did was to generate income for the current year or to deliver on the three-year management plan.

Investment banking is inherently transactional, with less emphasis on cultivating long-term relationships with suppliers and customers, unlike founder-led companies. As a result, these banks tend not to build on their brand's foundations but instead rely on cyclical rather than organic growth. Their expansion typically comes through transactions and acquisitions of other banks, or increased growth from the next wave of market activity.

What I learned in my time in investment banking was the importance of alignment and incentives. Humans have an innate desire to achieve, but as we will see later in this book, these ambitions can be distorted if the incentive structure is incorrectly applied and the time horizon excessively compressed. Although the approach in the investment banking world was in stark contrast to what I observed with the winemaker earlier in my career, it was invaluable to compare the two and see how meaningful behaviours propelled by the right motivations are key to the long-term destiny of a company.

By this point in my career, I had been exposed primarily to relatively large companies. It was not until I consulted to family offices that I gained an insider's appreciation for risk and the opportunity it could present.

Unlike the winemaker, which was an operating company, family offices have the expectation that risk comes with growth. One particular family office I worked with, founded by an accomplished businessman in his own right, had the ambition of building an endowment-style strategy focused purely on generating passive income that could fund its philanthropic endeavours in perpetuity. Through close collaboration with the family, I came to appreciate the importance of commercial judgement and the ability to take calculated risks. The family's goal of generating perpetual income drove them to pursue entrepreneurial opportunities and new revenue streams to sustain the necessary growth for the endowment. The focus, then, shifted to taking the right risks — making bold decisions that would yield significant long-term rewards.

For many of the founders I have met, making bold decisions is achieved by taking calculated risks where some form of competitive advantage already exists. Jack Gance, the co-founder of Chemist Warehouse, Australia's largest pharmacy chain, says he aims to 'enter into markets where I have the advantage. Never get into a fair fight or you'll both end up with bloody noses'.[1] That was the driving philosophy with which he grew to dominate the Australian pharmacy landscape. The lessons on risk-taking and correct decision-making would come to resonate with me, recurring time and time again with companies I would observe as an investor.

The three traits of great management teams

At its core, this book explores the question of value creation: Why do some companies evolve into wealth-generating engines, while others manage only short-lived growth before fading away? The essence of value creation lies in the series of decisions made by a company's leaders. These choices steer the organisation's course and define its future potential. Ultimately, it is the management team that drives value, determining which products and services to offer, formulating the strategies to win market share, and optimising the use of company resources. In their hands rest the fate of the business. This book explores the role of professional management teams, and by learning how to assess their effectiveness, we can gain the ability to foresee the success of any company.

It is worthwhile clarifying what is meant by value creation as it may mean different things to different organisations. *Value creation* in the context of this book is about *wealth creation*. This can take the form of earnings growth, dividend growth, and stock price appreciation. Exceptional management teams create great companies which, like a planet, attain their own gravitational force to attract talent, capital, customers, and therefore profits. Planets continue gathering their own momentum as they get bigger in size, collecting dust from space over millions of years. Great management teams nurture companies that, once set on the right path, continue snowballing in size by themselves and well into the future. And for those that get it right, the financial rewards for shareholders, management teams, and boards are life-changing—not to mention the value created via their products or services that meet or, even better, exceed consumer expectations.

Take for instance Hermès, the well-known French luxury brand. Founded in 1837 as a boutique harness-maker, the business has evolved from a saddlery in the 1800s into the luxury handbag and clothing company it is today. During that time, it has created immense wealth for its founding family, which today still owns 65 per cent of the available shares. At the end of 1994, it was valued with a market capitalisation of US$1.3 billion. Today, its market capitalisation is around US$220 billion—equivalent to a staggering annual compound growth rate of 19.3 per cent per annum (see figure I-1). In addition, shareholders have received significant dividend growth over time. Hermès's enduring value lies in its brand—it is not a company driven by fleeting trends. Instead, its business value is anchored in a strong brand strategy that will continue to generate wealth for its owners for many more years to come. This success has not been easy to come by; it is the culmination of sound management and long-term decisions that have firmly established Hermès as a symbol of luxury in consumers' minds. In other words, Hermès's current success is the product of an accumulation of wise management decisions made over many years.

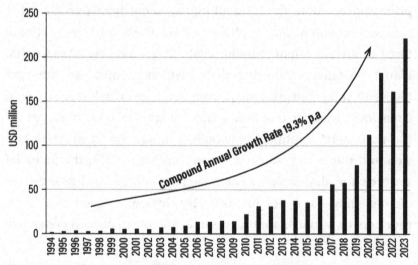

Figure I-1: Hermès's market capitalisation since IPO, 1994–2023.

Great companies come from diverse sectors and are led by management teams with varying philosophies and styles. The large body of research on management styles and techniques is directed towards professionals so they can employ them to improve their impact. This is a constantly evolving field in its own right, shaped by the ever-changing nature of human behaviour and societal expectations. However, this book is not focused on the nuances of management styles and skills; rather, it is the analysis and assessment of the results that we are interested in. And since we are focused on the outcomes delivered through a management team's skill, there are clear objective tests that can be applied across all sectors and styles to gauge the management team's potential to create long-term value.

At the end of the day, the role of management is to steer and grow the company to create long-lasting value. To do that, they need to demonstrate the capability for:

- Bold decision-making

- Motivation for the right reasons

- Commanding the masses.

Regardless of a company's industry or size, these three qualities are essential for effective management teams, forming the bedrock of long-term success and sustainable growth. Hermès exemplifies how the remarkable value created by such companies is deeply rooted in each generation of management upholding these principles.

Bold decision-making

There are specific moments in a company's history that present a fork in the road for management to decide whether to take a left or right turn. The correct choice generates value, while the wrong choice erodes value. Hermès experienced this in the 1990s when then-CEO Jean-Louis Dumas made the decision to phase out externally owned retail franchise stores while increasing the number of company-owned stores. In the short term this decision significantly increased capital expenditure and reduced sales volumes, but Dumas, being a member of the founding family, had the longer-term goal of elevating the in-store experience. He sought greater control over customer interactions with the brand—and despite the initial cost, the reduction in stores eventually generated an increased sense of exclusivity and brand cachet among customers, leading to an improvement in margins. This example underscores the value of eschewing rigid conventions in favour of a thoughtfully independent approach. In this instance, what appeared detrimental to the business in the short term was, in fact, the right decision for the long term. Dumas recognised the opportunity to elevate brand perception by limiting volume and enhancing the in-store experience, contrasting sharply with the prevailing strategy of broadening distribution and prioritising expansion. The effects of such decisions may not stand out with great significance by themselves but when stacked on top of each other and compounded over time, they begin sculpting a company's future.

Bold decision-making is not only based on independent logical deduction but having the fortitude to take calculated risks. Far too many bureaucratic companies fall into a culture frozen by conservatism at the board and management level. The appetite to take calculated risks then becomes lost in the aversion to venture off the beaten track, for fear that veering too far from benchmarked competitors automatically puts the company at risk. History is sprinkled with companies that have failed to move or have been too slow to adapt to changing technology (think Kodak or Blockbuster). We want management teams that take calculated risks and will change course if needed.

Nike was one of the earliest US companies to enter the Chinese market in 1981. Phil Knight, Nike's co-founder, had made the decision to begin manufacturing in China in the 1970s as he saw the large population, low wages, and talented workforce. Just as China was emerging from its decade-long Cultural Revolution and trade reopened, Phil Knight made use of Nike's already established manufacturing foothold by opening a marketing office, having negotiated its entry with the Chinese Communist Party by aligning itself with the government's ambition of economic growth and liberalisation. It was one of the first US companies to set up a local presence in China following the Cultural Revolution.[2] This was a bold move, but it was a move conducted with great consideration and thought. Phil Knight had observed that China's population was still on relatively low salaries and so the people were not ready to spend their discretionary income on sports shoes. What Nike needed to first promote were the sports it was most closely associated with, not the actual product itself. He believed that increasing China's engagement in sports would by osmosis benefit Nike's prospects. So it was with this logic that Nike opened in 1981 with a rather modest office of six employees dedicated to sponsoring and launching professional sporting leagues with a particular focus on basketball — a sport that Nike held a prominent association in through its sponsorships of top athletes, rather than the traditional expansion of store openings. Nike first had to create a culture of sport before customers could perceive the value of its shoes. The decision to move early into China and take a calculated risk paid off — over the next few decades, Nike progressed to become China's top sporting brand, riding the wave of its market leadership in basketball and its popularity as a sport in China.

However, this success proved fleeting as new competitors emerged, causing sales to stagnate from 2013 to 2014. The nature of success is that it attracts new entrants, prompting Nike's management team to make another bold decision. This time, drawing from its North America strategy, Nike sought to reposition itself as a premium brand, elevating itself from the mass market by raising prices and enhancing its in-store experience to target upper-middle-class customers. Essentially, it was prepared to forgo the mass market—a market increasingly crowded by competitors. By 2015, Chinese sales had improved 30 per cent as the brand's repositioning started to take hold, gaining acceptance among a cohort of the Chinese middle class seeking greater exclusivity (see figure I-2).

Nike's example demonstrates how bold decisions may not work out as originally planned, but it is necessary for management to have the conviction to step in and implement changes to correct, iterate, and improve their original decisions over time. Nike's management team was not frozen by conservatism but instead took calculated risks based on its observations of societal trends, adopting an approach bespoke to a specific market. It is the ability and conviction to make bold strategic decisions that defines great management.

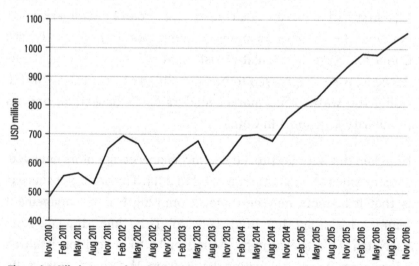

Figure I-2: Nike's quarterly sales in China, 2010–2016.

In Part 1 of this book, I will explore the science behind good decisions, and consider the key decision-making detractors and sources of errors in a team setting. I will also answer the questions:

- How are good decisions made?

- What key indicators can we use to identify management teams that excel in decision-making?

Motivation for the right reasons

The second hallmark of a great management team is its motivation being rooted in the right reasons. Most executives are propelled by a blend of personal interests—such as salary, career advancement, and prestige—and a genuine commitment to the company's success, particularly in delivering growth for shareholders. While some may be primarily driven by personal gain, others are prepared to make substantial sacrifices for the company's welfare. This balance becomes crucial, especially when the executives' personal interests conflict with the long-term goals of the organisation. In such cases, which motivation prevails?

Successful companies are led by individuals who prioritise collective success over personal gain, adopting a mindset akin to that of business owners. The distinction between executives motivated by personal benefit and those with an ownership mentality is subtle yet significant. To illustrate this point, consider the following scenario.

Imagine a company that has experienced several years of decline following a long period of success. Although it has only experienced the downturn for a relatively short period of time, the business remains profitable. The decline is a result of a reduction in product quality, rapid over-expansion, and competitors steadily taking market share. Despite these challenges, the business can manufacture growth by simply continuing to expand (and boost its revenues at the cost of reduced profitability) or by pursuing stock buybacks (which would boost the earnings per share). Both options offer quick fixes that secure executive KPIs and ensure remuneration bonuses, while also allowing executives to retain the appearance of career achievement, even if long-term sustainability may be compromised. The harder option is to deeply examine the reasons why the business is in decline and look to course correct, while accepting that this approach may risk a temporary reset in revenue over the short term.

The best way forward in this scenario may seem obvious when articulated in a few sentences; however, when put into this very scenario, many executives with, say, a seven-year term would not be willing to risk their own remuneration. For executives with an owner's mindset, the decision to deeply examine the business would be the sensible option and the preferred decision for the long term. This was the very choice Howard Schultz made when he returned to the Starbucks CEO position in 2008. What he returned to was a company that focused on financial metrics ahead of employee welfare, neglected to focus on barista training, and followed an ineffective expansion strategy that sacrificed product quality simply to increase the quantity of stores. As a result of a detailed review, he made drastic changes to correct the direction of the business. He shut down 600 under-performing stores, temporarily closed all US stores to upskill staff on fundamental coffee-making skills, settled a US$100 million legal dispute relating to back-tips for staff, and launched a loyalty program to rebuild trust with customers. It proved to be a difficult period, but those challenging times eventually paid off when the company was set back on track two years later—two long years that most other executives would not be willing to sacrifice.

Howard Schultz had been with Starbucks from its early days and helped to orchestrate its growth. When he returned to the business in 2008, he was a key shareholder—and he behaved as a founder would. As this example illustrates, the choices that shape a company are a result of the motivations that drive the key decision-makers. When a management team's motivations align closely with those of the business's owners, strategies and day-to-day decisions are more likely to focus on building long-term company value, rather than simply meeting executive KPIs for short-term bonuses and personal gain.

In Part 2 of this book, I will break down the components of executive-level motivation. I will share some examples of companies that have achieved great success by activating a wide array of motivators. And I will consider these fundamental questions:

- How can outsiders tell if a management team is closely aligned with owners/shareholders?

- How would an effective incentive scheme be structured to create alignment between management and shareholders?

- What are the fundamentals of assessing management incentive schemes?

Commanding the masses

No one person can do it all. Running a company successfully is a team effort. Leadership in this modern era involves more than just authority alone, but also inspiring and influencing others, engendering a sense of unity that drives teams toward achieving the strategic objectives set by the executive team. Executives who can inspire and influence are the ones who win the hearts and minds of employees, who then, in turn, give their best to achieve the goals that have been set before them.

In Part 3 of this book, we will explore the psychology behind effective teams and how to assess management's ability to exert influence through their own organisation. We will examine examples of companies that have scaled successfully with innovative organisational designs and those that have not, seeking answers to what structures enhance influence and why some companies perform better as they scale in size.

We will explore how executive teams can excel not only in influencing their employees but also in engaging customers and the broader community. Crafting a compelling company image and implementing strategies to attract and retain customers are vital. I will highlight the key elements of successful customer influence and how external observers can discern when these efforts are truly effective.

To understand how some teams rise to prominence, driving their businesses to unparalleled heights, I look at the following questions:

- What core principles lie at the heart of building lasting influence for a company?

- What are the telltale signs that a company is effectively leveraging its employees to bring its vision to life?

- How can we recognise when a management team is gaining traction and influence with its target markets?

As we uncover these answers, you will gain insights applicable to any organisation, along with the traits of influential management teams and their potential to create lasting success.

The Founder Framework

With the benefit of hindsight, identifying great management teams is easy—their success becomes the proof point of their abilities. But since it is much harder to look ahead to what has not yet happened, the real challenge for investors, executives, and board directors is to predict future performance.

The Founder Framework is a way of thinking about management teams to determine how effective they will be at creating value. It gives you the ability to make a realistic assessment based on past behaviours to determine if the management team is likely to create significant value over time (by exhibiting the qualities of a great team). The assessment is based on examining human behaviour and organisational dynamics. While management team members may not necessarily be founders, the Founder Framework determines how closely they behave like founders of the business.

A universal method of assessment

The Founder Framework measures the traits of great management teams:

- Can they make bold decisions?

- Are they driven by the right motivations?

- Can they command the masses?

The companies that exhibit the best of these qualities tend to be led by their founders, who lead their companies as an owner would. The more founder-like a management team is, the more aligned it is with delivering long-term results for shareholders.

There is no absolute requirement that the management team members must also be founders because as we will see, there are non-founder executives (professional managers) who have demonstrated these traits and been able to deliver extraordinary results.

By its very nature, judgement of people is difficult and fraught with subjectivity. That degree of subjectivity is enhanced further when it comes to teams, as not only are we assessing the performance and outlook of individuals, we are also assessing the attributes of the overall leadership team and how it interacts with employees. Add to this the corporate spin many executives are taught to weave (often a method to engender a sense of relatability with those they are attempting to influence) and very quickly the line of objectivity can be blurred when it comes to assessing management potential.

The Founder Framework will distinguish actions and outcomes as opposed to conjecture and aspirations. The Founder Framework focuses on factual observations, removing subjectivity and any emotional influence. Ideally, you want to avoid any undue influence from natural human biases. An assessment could be tainted if you have met executives in person (if you are an investor), if you work with them closely (if you are a board director), or if they are your management colleagues.

It is evident that some management teams consistently outperform others. The Founder Framework helps you identify the high performers. For investors, it serves as a crucial resource for evaluating management teams and gauging a company's potential. For board directors, the Framework provides a comprehensive method to uncover strengths and weaknesses within the executive team, enabling improvements in team motivation, KPI design, and the evaluation of judgement.

The three pillars

The three key traits used in the Founder Framework (see figure I-3) can be refined to three pillars when it comes to assessing the potential of management teams:

- **Judgement**—can they make bold and correct decisions?

- **Alignment**—are they driven by the same motivations as the owners of the company?

- **Influence**—can they win over their employees, customers, and the market?

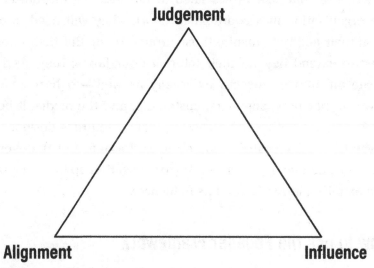

Figure I-3: The Founder Framework.

When it comes to **judgement**, management teams need to make the bold decisions in evolving business environments—they ultimately need to make the correct decisions, weighing which strategies they pursue and how they steer the company over the long term. There are no clear-cut answers, but their choices need to be the right ones.

The second pillar of the Framework, **alignment**, is an assessment of how well aligned management teams are with achieving their ultimate objective: to further the growth of the company for the benefit of its ultimate owners. Rather than being a test of pure motivation, which all C-suite managers possess in abundance, this is a test of cohesion between managers and owners. Is the management team behaving like a true owner of the business? Or is it a mere agent for the business? How can executive remuneration be constructed to motivate and align managers with shareholder goals? Are there any optimal ways to do this?

The third pillar is an assessment of **influence**. To be truly effective, C-suite executives need to harness the full power of the organisation in a coordinated effort. They will need to call upon their ability to inspire those around them. But their efforts need to extend beyond their internal boundaries; they need to create an aura of success externally as well—to harness the power of partners, suppliers, customers, and the media. It begs the question whether the organisational structure is designed in a way that enhances or hinders the performance of the overall company. Can management set the organisation up in such a way to maximise motivation and its influence?

How to use the Founder Framework

Each of the three pillars should be looked at separately. When combined together, we get an overall picture of the management team's expected performance in the future. Teams need to perform better than average across all three pillars, and they should be exceptional in at least two pillars to expect any meaningful success. Average does not work out. There are plenty of mediocre management teams around the world; to succeed over the long term requires exceptional abilities at a minimum.

As team composition naturally evolves, the Framework should be reviewed regularly, particularly during times of significant personnel changes. Companies experiencing major shifts in management or strategy require more frequent evaluations. In contrast, firms with stable leadership may not need assessments as often. However, even these stable teams should undergo periodic reviews to ensure they remain dynamic and do not risk becoming complacent or stagnant over time.

It is also natural for human behaviours to evolve and change over time rather than remain static. The motivation of people ebbs and flows depending on personnel, tenure, and the competitive environment. Remuneration packages that worked five years ago may not work today if the market environment has changed. For this reason, assessing management teams should be a regular exercise to ensure the company is always progressing and evolving with the shifting corporate environment.

PART I

Judgement

'Sound judgement comes from experience, and experience often comes from poor judgement.'
— **Anonymous**

When analysing a management team's potential, the question that needs answering is: How good is its judgement? How can we define judgement and everything it encompasses?

Great management teams make bold decisions. Sometimes these are extremely difficult decisions that have the potential to hurt the company in the short term—but if the choices are correct, the company grows. A new step change is achieved when a new product line is launched, when customer service is improved, or when the business is able to operate more efficiently – these outcomes stem from a company's ability to evolve with its customers and adapt to societal changes.

What distinguishes great management teams from merely adequate ones is a proven track record of delivering outcomes, showcasing their ability to make sound judgement calls not just in isolated instances, but consistently over time. The first pillar to indicate a high-performing management team in the Founder Framework is therefore the collective *judgement* of its members—decisions that generate optimal business outcomes for the organisation.

How can we assess judgement beyond looking backwards at results that have been achieved? What attributes provide clues to the judgement of management teams? A deeper examination of the core elements of judgement can offer an objective approach to assessing a management team's performance. These essential components can be effectively summarised and collectively evaluated using the Judgement Equation (figure P1-1, overleaf).

$$\text{Judgement} = \frac{\text{Decision Accuracy} + \text{Strategic Allocation}}{\text{Group Cognitive Biases}}$$

Figure P1-1: The Judgement Equation

We can make an objective assessment, over any defined period of time, of how well a management team exercises its collective judgement (using numbers if we want to be more mathematical) by reviewing the sum of the team's decision accuracy and its ability to allocate organisational resources to achieve strategic business goals, divided by a denominator—that being the group cognitive biases existing within the management team. The first two metrics are reasonably straightforward; however, for teams that wish to self-assess their judgement performance, a heightened level of self-awareness is required to identify cognitive biases that exist at the individual level and may permeate to the rest of the management team. External observers, though not privy to internal dynamics, can still identify subtle indicators and make informed deductions about the presence of cognitive biases within executive teams, as I will demonstrate in Chapter 3.

The components of the Judgement Equation will be explored in detail in the following chapters. For now, the key takeaway is that good judgement hinges on making accurate decisions and optimally allocating company resources. In contrast, cognitive biases that arise in group dynamics can undermine sound judgement when a team makes decisions.

Before we explore the Judgement Equation in detail, let me share the story of a generationally successful founder-led company that exemplifies the value of sound judgements made over the course of many decades.

The art of bold decisions

Our story begins in 1938 when a young man, who would later go on to be a business founder, returned to his home country following a few years away studying overseas. The international experience had given him a different take on life, one where he was able to witness how Japanese business was conducted, which was of great interest to him as he himself came from a wealthy Korean family that had established its riches through land ownership. The healthy stream of income from property leasing afforded him time to think about his future and explore opportunities without the immediate financial pressure of having to support his family. He was interested in entrepreneurship, though he did not have a particular industry he was passionate about. Even at this relatively young age, his sector-agnostic approach would become a hallmark trait that would serve him well in the future.

However, at this point in time, he was focused on starting something that could generate multiple sources of income. In that sense, he was an opportunist with an adaptive mindset when it came to business. Because of the scarcity of basic goods in his native country of Korea, he saw an opportunity to open a small trading business that imported and exported goods in his hometown. Luckily, he had the financial support of his family, who gifted him an amount of money equivalent to approximately US$8 million (in 2024 purchasing power dollars) — more than enough for him to get started. Slowly, he built the business from the ground up — first by importing and exporting items such as dried fish, noodles, and other groceries,[1] but eventually he expanded into producing his own brand of alcoholic beverages and packaged food. It was a prescient move as it allowed him to develop a manufacturing line, whereas previously he was warehousing and selling the goods of other companies.

It was the first instance of his decision-making accuracy that he would refine over decades, learning from mistakes and reflecting on what proved effective.

Through the 1940s, he worked to grow the business steadily, which was a credible achievement given the turbulence of those times in Korean history. At the time the country was in the midst of great political upheaval, with the north under the control of Soviet forces and the south under the control of US forces (all this came after decades of Japanese occupation until the end of the Second World War). We can only imagine the challenges of laying the foundations for a trading business against such a backdrop of confusion and with a lack of government policy stability. In fact, many wealthy families failed in their business ventures during this time, despite having the same if not more capital as our founder did. Wealth was no guarantee of success. In the end, when others saw risk, our founder saw opportunity.

By the skin of his teeth, he survived the Korean War in the 1950s and made the decision to relocate his business to Seoul to be closer to post-war reconstruction efforts. He also knew it would be a wise decision to be aligned physically and politically with the government powers, which would decide the most profitable trade contracts.[2] It was a move steeped with the recognition of an opportunity to position himself favourably with his now diversified trading and manufacturing business — a decision that would pay off handsomely as his business flourished under the inaugural post-war government.

The manner in which he secured favourable trade contracts with the government might not withstand today's stringent tender processes, but at the time, corporate regulation was not a priority for policymakers. They were often willing to make compromises for the sake of trade and economic growth.[2]

Our founder not only had a knack for recognising favourable conditions, but also the boldness to seize them. By the late 1950s, he had expanded his empire into textiles, construction, and food processing, transforming his business into one of the nation's largest enterprises, largely due to his close ties with the government. Yet, with this success came a growing — and ultimately precarious — dependence on those in power, a reliance that was about to unravel as the new decade approached.

When the Korean army staged a military coup in 1961, our founder knew he was in trouble. Not only did his steady flow of trade contracts cease, but he was also the target of an anti-corruption investigation by the incoming military government. Call it a stroke of luck or the art of smooth business deal-making, but somehow he managed to negotiate himself out of this precarious situation. He promised to help the incoming government achieve its vision of establishing Korea as an Asian manufacturing powerhouse — to move away from a focus on trading raw materials and turn towards becoming a value-adding economy that would rank among Asia's top exporters. In return, the new government agreed to overlook any past misdeeds. Only a few companies at the time had the extensive production capacity and connections internationally that could help the government, which would prove to be a key factor in why the military government chose to negotiate with our founder. It was his earlier decision to expand broadly that helped avert his potential downfall.

With the renewed sense of purpose to align itself with the economic growth of the country, the company diversified further over the course of the 1950s and 1960s. It established and invested in businesses related to wool-spinning, chemicals, fertilisers, shipbuilding, and paper manufacturing — strategically chosen by the founder to capitalise on government policy at the time. But there were two bold decisions that would elevate the company from being a national champion into an international household brand. The first was the establishment of a sugar refiner called Cheil Jedang, now known as CJ. This business has today evolved into a leading global food producer — a multi-billion-dollar listed company that remains majority-owned by the founding family. The second was a decision to start manufacturing black-and-white TVs in 1969.

I will take a brief pause here as at this point you may have an inkling about who the founder and the company might be. Up until this point of the story, the history of this company is almost unrecognisable from what it is today. That is because Lee Byung-Chull, our founder (Figure P1-2), did not set out intending to build Samsung into a global electronics powerhouse. It was rather a series of judgement calls that led the business he founded to pursue this sector. Lee once said: 'The only way a company could win in competition is through logical decision-making, which enables it to cut costs and produce affordable and good quality products. This is why it is always important to introduce systems from advanced nations and develop technologies, which are critical to improving business management.'[3]

It was with this mindset that the trajectory of the company changed, with the establishment of Samsung Electronics in 1969. The company moved from crowded, commoditised industries into a cutting-edge segment where it would face less competition. It was not simple though. The move also required a significant amount of capital to construct electronic manufacturing lines and develop new supply chains. But it had the support of government. After all, Samsung was earmarked to be a champion of industry that would lift Korea out of its economic doldrums.

If we appraise Lee Byung-Chull's judgement in terms of the Judgement Equation, his decision accuracy was high—moving into food manufacturing in Samsung's early days, followed by expansion into electronics in the 1970s proved to be a masterstroke that would reap rewards for decades to come. The shift to electronics marked the first step in transforming the company from a television manufacturer into a diversified brand of household appliances and white goods.

The decision to start Samsung Electronics led to another bold move in the 1980s. With its success moving into household electronics, Lee Byung-Chull wanted to further elevate his company (and the country) by moving even closer to the cutting edge of technology. He could see the semiconductor industry[4] was becoming a critical link in the development of the personal computer, which was beginning to accelerate in the US. So, he decided to rethink the direction of the company again, putting aside significant portions of its profit to fund the research and development of semiconductors. It turned out not only to be an accurate decision, but a clever use of strategic capital allocation. By leveraging the company's already-established manufacturing infrastructure and research teams, Samsung was able to minimise the risk of its new venture.

It would be remiss to overlook the third component of the Judgement Equation: cognitive biases. Samsung is by no means a perfect company. Its deficiencies have only been masked by the many decades of accurate decisions and excellent strategic allocation that have propelled it to success. In the 1990s, Samsung products experienced a decline in desirability.[5] The company had expanded overseas, only to realise its products were falling short in quality compared to other international brands, a consequence of the management's complacency after years of success. Cognitive biases within the leadership team led to a period of stagnation, despite efforts to re-evaluate the company's strategy. Additionally, being family-controlled added another layer of complexity, with personal relationships and decision-making biases further complicating matters. For example, the founder's second son was ostracised by the family after embezzling funds in the 1960s. He was subsequently removed from Samsung, never to return again. In 2017, the grandson of the founder and chair of Samsung Electronics was convicted of bribery and jailed.

Despite its controversies and missteps,[6] Samsung has continued to evolve and grow. What can we learn from Samsung's imperfect journey to global leadership? It reveals that sound judgement lies in making bold, accurate decisions and efficiently allocating strategic resources. While there were cognitive flaws in the decision-making process, these were outweighed by earlier bold moves that steered the company in the right direction, allowing Samsung to progress and offset any deficiencies. In Samsung's case, many key decisions were shaped by the founder's vision and business philosophy. His ability to influence the company without the constraints of corporate bureaucracy undoubtedly led to the game-changing creation of Samsung Electronics, which today remains the jewel in its crown.

Figure P1-2: Samsung's founder Lee Byung-Chull.

Samsung's journey is just one example of a founder-led success story that illustrates the value of the Judgement Equation. In the following chapters, I step you through each of the components of the Judgement Equation to fully explain what they mean.

CHAPTER 1

Decision accuracy

Sound decision-making involves making optimal choices in the face of competing constraints and varying time horizons. The results may not be immediately clear within a year or two; it takes patience for initiatives to gain traction within the organisation and for customers to adapt to the changes. But stack enough of these optimal decisions together over the longer term and the weight of correct judgement begins to create momentum that snowballs in favour of the company. Along the way, the management team will have left behind a trail of footprints as a record of its decisions.

Steering the ship in the right direction

There are two angles from which to approach an assessment of a management team's decision-making accuracy. First, you need to consider the key questions being asked of management and the challenges the team had to overcome. The management team would have proposed its strategy to address these challenges, whether it be related to macro conditions, competitors, or adapting to new customer needs. These would usually be outlined in strategic investor updates and annual reports. Alongside these challenges, management would have outlined its approach and solution. Both the purported challenges and subsequent solutions are important sources of information that allow you to discern whether the direction taken by management proved successful. The challenges cited by management serve as the rationale for why certain strategic directions were taken. With any company, there will always be challenges (that is the very nature of business). By understanding the context of the history of these challenges, you can discern whether management succeeded in overcoming these challenges and making progress, or whether the challenges became prolonged issues that have hampered long-term growth. This is why it is necessary to establish a meaningful record of decision-making by delving back through three to five years of company records.

The second angle to consider is the output of management decisions. You are looking for the results — how effective were the decisions? There should be supporting evidence the company is progressively being steered in the right direction. This evidence can come from the following:

- **Financial performance.** It will likely take more than one year for strategic decisions to flow through to the bottom line, though eventually you can expect improved financial metrics in the form of increasing revenue, cashflow generation, margins, or in the case of efficiency-drive decisions, streamlining of operational costs. If the business has been able to produce consistent growth over a few years, then the decisions made in years prior have paid off.

- **Delivery of strategic projects.** Progress can be objectively measured by the resultant delivery of strategic projects. For example, management teams that aim to expand into overseas markets would have secured a joint venture partnership arrangement, opened up new facilities, completed an acquisition, or established a distribution agreement. These are observable facts that point to progress being made.

- **Winning market share.** Increasing market share is a clear sign that management have created a compelling product or service that customers perceive as superior to others available in the market. As a result of management action, the product being offered either has better features, improves customer service, or has a pricing advantage. Market share data is attainable through research reports or can be approximated by aggregating total sales from the company and its key competitors.

- **Internal and external satisfaction.** Net Promoter Scores and employee satisfaction ratings are not only results of internal and external satisfaction but also reflect the output of management strategies that have been rolled out. Well-executed initiatives ensure employees are aligned and on board. Engaged employees who are happy in their roles perform more effectively and generate greater customer satisfaction. Net Promoter Scores, if available, can indicate if good decisions have been made with how front-line teams have been structured. Equally, the results of employee satisfaction surveys (or other online portals that allow employees to comment on management) provide some insight into how employee-related decisions impact on the performance of the company.

From my experience, I caution against placing too much weight in online portals that all employees can use to comment on management. Firstly, disgruntled employees are usually more vocal than happy ones. Secondly, isolated pockets of dissatisfied employees could be the by-product of a restructure or reallocation necessary to improve the business. The perception of employees, given their subjective nature, may not be indicative of management's decision-making.

In the following case studies, I contrast two large multinational companies to show the differences in approach through adversity. One company continues to struggle as it grapples with the chronic tendency of applying short-term patches for systemic problems, whereas another rewires its thinking and takes on responsibility for a permanent solution. Let us start with an examination of Boeing and its recent challenges.

Persistent issues: Boeing[1-3]

In 2020, Boeing, one of the world's leading aerospace manufacturers, suffered a crisis that would lead to the death of 346 people, its largest ever quarterly loss, the resignation of its chair, the firing of key executives, including the CEO, a lawsuit settlement with investors, and reputational damage that would hinder sales for years to come. All this despite possessing world-class business leaders in its management team and board. This was a failure of execution and decision-making involving the most experienced individuals in the aerospace manufacturing industry.

The failure stemmed not from individual shortcomings but from mismanagement at the board and executive levels, highlighting that strong individuals don't always make effective teams. The root cause was the competitive pressure from rival Airbus, which had just introduced the fuel-efficient A320neo. Meanwhile, Boeing was heavily invested in its 787 Dreamliner program, already three years behind schedule. The chair at the time remained convinced that the company's future hinged on the success of the Dreamliner. Being already a few steps behind its rival, there was growing pressure from customers to rectify and catch up. Boeing executives debated whether doubling down on the 787 Dreamliner was worth it, or whether they should consider repurposing an already-existing design as the quickest way to catch up. Since significant investments had already been made to rectify the 787 Dreamliner program, management made the decision to continue to invest in the program.

Not long after the management team had decided on its strategy, one of Boeing's most loyal and longstanding customers, American Airlines, advised that it had decided to leave Boeing and sign up to order rival Airbus's new A320neo plane. It was a surprise to the management team and had the potential to cascade to other clients. Here was an American customer that had chosen a French supplier over a long-standing relationship with an American company. American Airlines represented a significant slice of revenue, which Boeing did not want to lose. However, Boeing was not able to compete quickly with Airbus. The bad news hit while Boeing was already on the defensive, intensifying the pressure on its management. The team found itself in an increasingly precarious situation.

In response, Boeing decided to reverse the path it had chosen with the 787 Dreamliner. Management needed to quickly meet the demands of customers, and the already-delayed 787 program would take too long to deliver. Instead, the management team decided to redivert its resources to repurposing the tried-and-tested 737 aircraft—a bestseller with over 50 years of proven safety records. From the management team's perspective, it was faster to adapt the older design in a way that would meet current safety and testing standards than to persevere with the troubled 787 Dreamliner project.

Boeing's management team scrambled and pleaded with American Airlines to consider a new proposal: divert some of American Airlines' new orders from the Airbus A320neo to Boeing, with the promise that Boeing would deliver an updated 737 MAX on time, including up-to-date safety standards and retaining the familiar controls so pilots would only require minimal extra training. Eventually, American Airlines agreed to split its order between Airbus and Boeing on the condition the updated 737 MAX would be delivered on time and to the specifications promised. Thus, the Boeing 737 MAX was born under a fire of expectation and anticipation.

The elements that contribute to Boeing's myopic decision-making were set: an extreme focus to recoup short-term revenues, and poor planning to fully understand the implications of each strategic option. Although the individuals on the executive team were highly experienced, the resultant failures were errors of coordination and teamwork, which layered upon and compounded each other. The end result of these management mistakes was a rushed design project cobbled together in an attempt to win back lost customers. Due to the older 737 MAX design template, a myriad of adjustments needed to be made to accommodate a newer engine—all to keep up with the improved fuel efficiency of its competitor, the Airbus A320neo. These adjustments included new manoeuvring software that auto-corrected the angle of the aircraft's nose and allowed it to meet safety requirements. Ultimately it would be this software that would fail and lead to the crash of two flights, killing a total of 346 people, as well as the subsequent investigation, which would reveal the failures of Boeing's management team.

Given the urgency of the 737 MAX project, it was important to Boeing's financial results that the testing and correction process was completed quickly so that aircraft safety requirements could be met with minimal delay. In the investigation following the aftermath of the crash and grounding of the 737 MAX, journalists exposed that Boeing's managers rejected multiple upgrades suggested by engineers during the testing process. Pressure was instead applied to keep all the flight instruments the same as the older model, which would avoid the need for further pilot training and appease customer preferences.

Questions were also raised about the oversight and accountability of the 737 MAX project. The decision-making process was imbalanced and did not consider the significant risks of the design, as the management team's thought processes were focused primarily on meeting deadlines and customer preferences. Dennis Muilenburg, who started with Boeing as an intern in 1985 and had risen through the ranks to become Chair and CEO, was eventually terminated. The executive management team, despite impressive individual accomplishments, was criticised for a lack of transparency while handling the investigation. It was slow to communicate with regulators and the public. Boeing's systemic failures in leadership, governance, and corporate culture within the company were exposed. The lack of effective oversight, transparency, and accountability at the highest levels of management exacerbated the severity of the crisis and undermined trust in Boeing's ability to prioritise safety and deliver a reliable aircraft to its customers.

Contrary to popular belief, identifying great management teams isn't as straightforward as it seems. Unlike student test scores, which provide an immediate and objective measure of effort, corporate performance unfolds over much longer periods. Executives don't face a single final exam; rather, they undergo countless mini-tests over the years. The results of these cumulative tests form the foundation on which management teams are ultimately judged.

Take Boeing's saga, for instance. The company's series of missteps began with the troubled 787 Dreamliner — plagued by delays and poor execution. Then came the abrupt pivot, a knee-jerk reaction to the loss of a key customer. In a rushed attempt to stay competitive, Boeing hastily resurrected the 737 MAX, cutting corners to meet deadlines. Under immense pressure, mistakes mounted, and one poor decision led to another, eventually culminating in disaster. This catastrophe exposed a long history of flawed judgement, but the tests had been submitted years earlier — only since that fateful day have the true results come to light.

In contrast to the Boeing example, the experience of Siemens shows us how adversity can be managed successfully through considered decision-making that can reset the company's prospects. Whereas Boeing's challenges were prolonged through a failure of decision-making, the following case study demonstrates how Siemens' recovery was architected by sound choices that started from the very top and flowed through the entire organisation.

Genuine change: Siemens[4-7]

In the field of engineering and digital technology, one must be at the cutting edge of developments in order to remain competitive. This requires a level of constant reinvention, a challenge for many large corporations that often rest on their laurels, relying on profitable divisions until they are close to extinction, instead of looking ahead for the next source of innovation.

Siemens was always able to anticipate the next wave of technological advancement. It was never in its DNA to rest on its laurels. It had developed an outstanding reputation as a German engineering company with business lines in electrical networking, white goods, medical technology (including x-ray devices), telecommunication devices, and networks. The company's stellar reputation epitomised the global esteem for German engineering. Its standing had been developed since its founding in the 1800s. For over a century, the company expanded and built its reputation for reliability and precision.

That was until 2006, when — to the shock and surprise of Siemens' board — German regulators raided the headquarters of its head office and charged Siemens with corruption and bribery. At first, Siemens had the impression this was an isolated case, with minimal reputational and financial impact. As the investigation unfurled, the extent of the bribery uncovered was anything but trivial. Regulators uncovered evidence that systemic bribery had taken place within the organisation — so much so that Siemens employees understood the accounting entry called 'useful expenditures' as being a well-known hidden reference to bribes. Hidden bank accounts, obscure entities and fictional consultants had been used to obfuscate bribery payments to customers in the quest to win business and meet sales targets.

The consequences of these findings were significant for Siemens. Not only did the investigation inflict reputational damage on this bastion of German business, but Siemens also received a record US$1.6 billion fine and experienced the loss of its Chair and CEO in the aftermath of its internal investigation. When the hunt for a new CEO yielded the first externally hired CEO in its long history, further key personnel were sacked, including 80 per cent of the managing board, 70 per cent of the next tier of senior staff, and 40 per cent of the next level below that. A mass clean-out and streamlining of the organisation was implemented.

At the time, Siemens' future was bleak as it faced increasing global competition and rapid advancements in technology, which brought with them the need to evolve internal systems and a continual demand for research and development expenditure to create the latest cutting-edge products that customers expected. Meanwhile, there was a complex governance board system that comprised two layers — a supervisory board and a management board. Below that were operating CEOs in charge of operational units.

History is littered with global corporations that have never recovered from such a crisis. For most, a recovery would not be guaranteed, and even if it was within the realm of consideration, such a recovery would take years. However, it was through strong management planning and execution that Siemens recovered quickly. Its new (outsider) CEO formed a fresh eight-person managing board, reducing the number from 12. The consolidated number was designed to reflect a more streamlined approach to decision-making and allow for adaptations to the changing market. *To be battle-ready, one needs the right army for the conditions.*

Siemens centralised the business further, and the number of total divisions shrunk as it reimagined the organisational design across the 190 countries in which it operated. Importantly, these changes were implemented without the input of third-party consultants. The CEO at the time reasoned that it was only internal management that could solve the problems — they were the only ones close enough to appreciate their own needs and accountabilities.

Fast-forward to today, and Siemens' share price has more than tripled since the crisis. It has reinvented itself as an innovative engineering company, aligning itself to the key industries relevant to today's world, including renewable energy, digital infrastructure, healthcare, and advanced manufacturing. This transformation has come at significant research and development cost, dragging short-term profits lower with the intention of generating longer-term benefit. It has also required the reshaping of its management priorities: spending more time meeting customers and gathering intelligence on which key industry trends will lead to more business down the road.

The outcome of Siemens' reinvention led it to focus on three new pillars that would underpin Siemens' growth over the next decade: the creation of a sustainability portfolio, a refocus on infrastructure, and increased spending on innovation research and development.

Siemens is an example of a large organisation that has turned itself around from crisis within a short timeframe. The catalyst for this turnaround was a reset of company focus and a change of management leadership — both through reducing executive numbers and reinventing the governance structure. These decisions have proven valuable over time. Siemens' management team has made well-considered but bold decisions, a feat made more challenging in large bureaucratic organisations spanning almost every country in the world. These decisions have altered the fortunes of a global giant that could have very well joined the history books as another ageing dinosaur (figure 1-1 shows Siemens' recovery from its 2006 crisis).

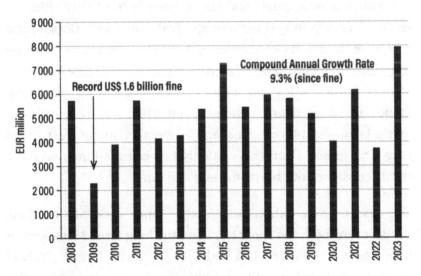

Figure 1-1: Siemens' net profit, 2008–2023.

Future impact

Not many management teams have the staying power to see out their decisions. Usually those that do will have a closer relationship to the business beyond just a salary and bonus package. For example, founders will often care more about the long-term growth of a company and be more likely to remain involved to see their decisions come to fruition. This level of longevity is rare and, as we will explore in Chapter 5, the identification of this trait requires first an understanding of the psychological aspects of human motivation. The reason why corporate longevity is so rare is because management teams constantly face the opposing forces of choosing what is good for the company in the long term versus what will generate short-term results. What generates the best results in the short term may in fact be detrimental to the company in the long term. For example, Yahoo! was the leader in internet search, email, and online news in the 1990s[8,9] but has let that lead slip to new technology rivals Microsoft, Google, and Facebook. Unlike its competition, Yahoo! neglected to focus on hiring and developing talented programmers to improve its core suite of products. Instead, Yahoo! chose to focus on generating immediate advertising revenues, diverting its resources to maximising short-term gains and neglecting to reinvest in its long-term future. Decisions can only be accurate if management teams consider both horizons near and far.

The lesson from Yahoo! shows the importance of balancing decisions for both the short term and the long term. Management teams need to be correct in both time horizons. In 2006, Yahoo! made a US$1 billion offer to buy Facebook but was swiftly rebuffed. As Mark Zuckerberg, co-founder and CEO of Facebook recalls, there was immense pressure internally from employees and executive management to sell the business to Yahoo! and capitalise on a huge windfall gain—many of them had stock options and would have been paid out handsomely. But Mark Zuckerberg saw the opportunity to expand Facebook beyond the student market—it was a long-term decision that went against the wishes of many senior executives who wanted a short-term payout. In the end, Yahoo!'s takeover bid was rejected by Mark Zuckerberg. That decision would prove to be a long-term winner though not without short-term unpopularity—in a vote of disappointment at no longer being able to realise their valuable stock options, all of Facebook's senior management team left the business within a year of the failed takeover. Mark Zuckerberg's decision not to sell proved to be correct in the end—Facebook (now Meta) is now worth well over US$1 trillion.

As the Yahoo! example shows, a myopic focus on the short term blinds a management team's ability to make bold long-term decisions. To make accurate decisions, management teams need to pay heed not just to the *now* but also to the *next*. Those with blinkers on will be destined to fail eventually.

Look for clues that paint a picture of how a management team thinks. Even outsiders can gain insight by stitching together these clues to determine a management team's frame of mind. For starters, the dividend payout ratio (the proportion of dividends paid out from profits) indicates the level of cash that is returned back to investors—the greater the payout ratio, the less cash is retained within the business for future growth. Excessive payout ratios (80 per cent or more) often indicate the company is in 'cash-cow' mode and is simply looking to generate cash. An example is IBM, which paid out 80 per cent or more of its earnings in every year between 2020 and 2023 (in some years it has dipped into cash reserves to achieve this as dividends paid out have exceeded earnings).[10] When a company is in cash-cow mode, it seeks to maintain a high constant dividend with little regard for the natural fluctuations of business. This means management teams are focused on maintaining short-term returns to ensure they can continue delivering the level of dividends their shareholders have come to expect. Coca-Cola is another example that has paid out dividends in the range of 74–94 per cent of its earnings during the period from 2014 to 2023.[10] These management teams rely on existing business models that continue generating profits but pay little attention to creating new engines of growth for the future.

Similarly, research and development (R&D) and capital expenditure (capex) costs as a percentage of revenues indicate a management team's intent at investing into the future to stay in the front of its field. R&D and capex are investments that do not offer instant gratification. They create an immediate monetary cost to the business, but their benefits are backended—in other words, realised over many years. To gain a sense of reasonableness, it is useful to compare R&D and capex (as a percentage of revenues) across competitors to form an approximate benchmark. The aim is to establish a sense of each management team's time horizon, and to ensure they are not myopic in their outlook. The accuracy of a company's decisions depend on the management team's ability to optimise the company for its short-term requirements and its long-term ambitions.

The best defence is offence

Decision accuracy requires a willingness to take on a defensive mindset when required, but also to be comfortable with the inherent uncertainty in the pursuit of growth that is required in business. Too often, management teams make bad decisions because they are fixated on preserving their existing business rather than evolving their business within changing environments. Accurate decisions cannot be made with a solely risk-averse stance. This is because a mindset of avoiding failure inevitably ignores the full universe of decisions available to management teams. How can decisions be accurate if they have not considered the full gamut of possibilities? Management teams that underestimate changes in technology, competitor actions, and changing customer expectations assume that defending their turf in the same way as before is the correct approach to take. This ignores the fact that the basis for their assumptions may be incorrect; that is, technological developments, rising competition, and the evolution of customer expectations are not static. Since these are areas prone to dynamic change, a company needs to be able to adapt to these shifting foundations pre-emptively. The best management teams see offence as the best form of defence.

Marks & Spencer (M&S), a major UK fashion retailer, has lost significant ground over the years to H&M, Zara, and Uniqlo because of its decision in the 2000s to cut costs by closing stores, reducing its workforce, and reducing spending on technology and new store formats. This led to a downward spiral in its offering to customers. In effect, M&S shrunk its business to protect what it had, when in fact it was missing out on opportunities to transform its business for the future. M&S failed to invest in supply chain efficiency, it missed the rise of ecommerce, and it continued to operate on a slow design cycle that failed to adapt to changing customer tastes. In recent years, M&S has fallen well behind its competitors in clothing; instead, its attention has shifted to the online grocery and delivery segment via its 50 per cent joint venture with Ocado in 2019. An overly defensive mindset in the 2000s resulted in M&S losing its lead in the clothing sector, which forced its hand and led to its pursuit of a different market.

Contrast M&S's experience with Zara (see figure 1-2, overleaf), which was only founded in 1975 (M&S was founded in 1884). Zara

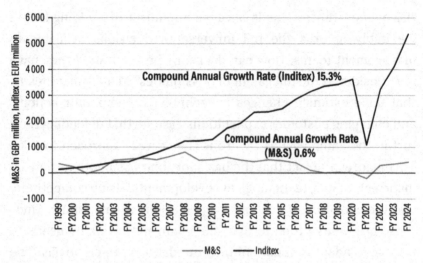

Figure 1-2: Net profit for Marks & Spencer versus Inditex (parent company of Zara), 1999–2024.

has surpassed M&S by taking an offensive mindset, continually investing in accelerating supply chain logistics and its design cycle. As the technology era emerged, Zara embraced newly available technologies to enhance its inventory management, integrating real-time data on design, production, and retail to speed up its reaction time to customer trends. Zara was among the first fashion retailers to leverage mobile apps and explore digital channels as a way to engage and sell to its customers.

To be clear though, Inditex (which is Zara's listed company owner) remains a conservatively managed business with minimal debt and a strong financial position. Inditex has embraced an offensive strategy without compromising its defensive stance. Its approach to decision-making incorporates both defensive and offensive thinking, leading to more complete and accurate decisions than those of a purely defence-minded management team, such as M&S's.

Organisations that engage exclusively in cost-cutting strategies stand to lose more ground over the long term. For evidence of bold decision-making, look for management teams with a trend-setter mentality—they may be looking to develop cutting-edge products, adopting the use of new tools and systems, or developing a unique brand to differentiate themselves from the competition. These management teams seek to improve outcomes for customers. Therefore, a key question to ask when assessing a management team is: Are the changes that are being implemented aimed at improving the outcomes for customers?

Outsiders can see this through observing the company's products and its strategic initiatives. Are products being developed that fill a need for customers? Are they being brought to market faster and more efficiently? Is the customer experience smoother? Steer clear of companies whose decision-making is compromised by a trend-follower mentality—their focus will turn towards benchmarking against the competition rather than improving their products and services for the betterment of society and their customers. Rather than *setting* the benchmark, these management teams miss opportunities (as we have seen with Yahoo! and M&S) because they are too focused on *following* the benchmark and matching competitors.

CHAPTER 2

Strategic allocation

To demonstrate strong judgement, decision-making needs to be accurate, but accuracy is not the only crucial factor—*how* these decisions will be executed is of equal importance. This is the second component of the Judgement Equation—the ability of management teams to strategically allocate capital and people to pursue their value-adding initiatives. Being resourceful so decisions can come to fruition is just as critical to good judgement as the decision itself.

Every organisation, regardless of the size of the business, has the same two resource buckets to evaluate and deploy in its efforts to achieve business objectives: capital and people. Great management teams extract maximum productivity, efficiency, and output by optimising these two core resources to achieve the most bang for buck. They have a resourcefulness that enables them to make the most of what is available. Sounds simple enough until you throw in competing interests and the limitations of resource scarcity across the buckets.

I had a conversation once with a founder of a publicly listed financial services firm who shared with me his strategy for growing his business. He described to me the opportunity he saw in the early 2000s when IT systems first became widespread in his industry. Back then, customer relationship management was not at all centralised, but rather managed by teams of salespeople that shared contacts via spreadsheets and internal updates. When he recognised this trend and could see the benefits of a central information repository, he much preferred to reinvest company profits into upgrading the IT system rather than hiring more sales managers (which was what his competitors were doing). He recalled to me a story of his middle management team wanting more budget to hire additional personnel. With a wry smile, he explained his strategy of deliberately leasing a smaller office space (at the time he was employing 300 people) with very few spare desks. He told me, 'The less spare desks people see, the less they will feel the need to hire.' He was looking to take the company in another direction. He was allocating capital to in-house software, not salaries and wages. Decades later, the in-house software turned out to be a significant revenue generator as it evolved into a proprietary tool that could be licensed for external use.

Inefficiencies and wastage are more common than optimised outcomes. Executives are constantly adjusting and (oftentimes) competing with one another for resources—this is not an issue, rather just a reality of an organisation's budgeting process. The story usually goes like this: The annual budgeting process kicks off, where senior leaders are asked to put together their proposed budget 'asks' for the next fiscal year. Depending on the economy at the time, this process may come with a spiel about clamping down on expenditure; however, in good times, capital may be squandered on ambitious projects that draw significantly on a company's people resource, or on acquisitions that simply increase the size of a company but fail to add to its profitability.

Decision accuracy is the ability to make the correct calls, while strategic allocation is the ability to harness both the financial and people power to enhance the outcome. Management teams that exhibit sound judgement always seem to strategically make the most of the capital and people at their disposal. So how can we identify good strategic resource allocation?

Harnessing capital for strategic impact

The strategic use of capital goes beyond merely supporting business operations; it becomes a powerful tool for growth and compounding. Rather than viewing capital as just a resource used to fund operations, it can instead be leveraged to expand the company's assets over time. While many might be content to harvest the fruit from a tree regularly, keeping it the same size, management teams that prioritise nurturing the tree will see it yield more fruit each year. Eventually, the tree grows so large that it becomes a formidable asset in itself, allowing the company to wield its full financial strength as a strategic advantage.

In the following sections, I take you through an example of a company that has been able to achieve extraordinary growth through the effective use of its capital. This success has been achieved within the confines of an industry (insurance) typically seen as boring and slow-growing. Even within this regulated environment, this US-based insurer has been able to turn US$1000 invested 30 years ago into US$3 545 800 today. This staggering gain is based on its stock price appreciation and the dividends that it has paid out to investors over its history (see figure 2-1, overleaf).

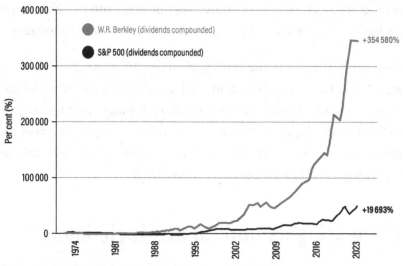

Figure 2-1: W.R. Berkley cumulative total return, 1973-2023.

Building a compounding asset pool

In the beginning, W. R. Berkley did not have much capital. But management knew it had to accumulate it gradually if it was to compete with much larger insurance companies. William Berkley, its founder, explained that the company's strategy was to adopt a conservative capital approach and ensure it remained in the game by always having an excess buffer for any worst-case scenario.[1] This meant forgoing quick gains, instead focusing on taking the premium income it would receive and investing it into government bonds. The rates on these bonds were just enough to generate a small excess income every year, even after paying out insurance claims. And because insurance claims are inherently volatile, the capital had to be kept readily available in case there was a bad year with many claims. The excess income generated by the bonds was stored away—just like a coin-by-coin approach with a piggy bank. As at 2023, W. R. Berkley had accumulated US$25 billion in investment capital that generated US$1 billion in investment income for shareholders. The income has been used to pay dividends continuously since 1976 and reinvested back into the business as retained profits—this explains how the capital base has compounded over time, creating a virtuous cycle of greater income and greater reinvestment.

What W. R. Berkley has demonstrated is the clever use of capital as a tool to generate additional income. This first requires the management team to recognise the importance of retaining capital and not squandering it on 'empire building' activities, and secondly to reinvest capital in a considered way that does not seek to maximise gains, but rather to accumulate gains incrementally. If capital is being well managed by a management team, you can expect to see cash building up gradually over years and being reinvested in low-risk financial instruments. Conversely, if capital is not being managed effectively, you can expect to see evidence of large amounts of cash being blown on large acquisitions, leading to the level of management compensation skyrocketing, an investment in excessively large and lavish office spaces, and the hiring of increasing numbers of third-party consultants and marketing agencies. These are all ways in which management teams waste capital simply because they see an increasing cash balance and feel the tendency to maximise its use. Instead, companies like W. R. Berkley see excess cashflow as a resource that can bolster its financial foundations and be added to its income-generating toolkit.

Managing debt

Even with a large cash balance, W. R. Berkley utilises debt to provide funding stability to preserve cash buffers and fund growth initiatives. But it manages its borrowings conservatively. Throughout its history, it has maintained a low and steady amount of debt at a constant ratio to its capital base, and has spread the debt across different maturities. By limiting the amount of debt it uses, the interest burden is ringfenced and capped. And by spreading the borrowing maturities, there is no single large tranche of debt that needs to be repaid in any given year, which removes any significant pressure should market conditions change. As the business generates significant cash from its operations, the debt burden is more than easily covered by the income being generated each year. The purpose of the debt is to add extra capital reserves and allow a buffer to pursue expansion opportunities into new geographies and insurance lines.

In my experience working in capital markets, I have observed many executive teams underestimate the time required to manage debt effectively. This process can be a significant distraction from more value-adding initiatives. Negotiating debt terms with bondholders or lenders often involves extensive discussions through bankers, roadshows, and tours to generate interest, and substantial fees paid to bankers and lawyers to coordinate these efforts. Executives are often wined and dined throughout this process, and those who enjoy the indulgence opt to repeat it every few years by refinancing.

While taking on debt has its benefits—such as increased tax efficiency, favourable interest rates that lower the company's overall cost of capital, and securing long-term financing to meet future needs—I have noticed that the time commitment can be substantial. Managing debt is only worthwhile if the value of the additional funding outweighs the opportunity cost—the potential benefits that could be realised if executives focused on other growth initiatives. Unfortunately, this trade-off is often overlooked by many management teams.

Executive teams with a good eye for strategic allocation will use debt sparingly and within certain boundaries to preserve their headspace for more important matters.

Allocating capital for acquisitions and organic growth

In the early decades from 1970s to 1990s, W. R. Berkley made a series of niche acquisitions that transformed its business from an investment management firm into an insurance and reinsurance business. The strategy of these early acquisitions was to buy niche insurers in specialised lines of business. This included a property and casualty insurer (a line of insurance which covers against property damage and liability) that specialised in regional Texas locations, followed by Union Insurance, which had a foothold in Nebraska. It was not only seeking geographic niches but also custom insurance businesses that insured for specific risks (for example, commercial liability insurance—which covers any damage caused during business operations). At the time, W. R. Berkley could not compete with the mega insurers with huge swathes of capital, so it had to instead focus on buying niche, specialised, and targeted acquisitions that did not require large amounts of capital.[2] These insurers would be market leaders in their specialised field, have high levels of profitability and attractive margins—they possessed better quality but with less scale as compared to the large diversified insurance groups. By bolting on many of these smaller businesses one piece at a time, W. R. Berkley effectively achieved scale without having to make one super-sized acquisition.

The business today has 60 individual subsidiary companies, of which seven were acquired (mainly during the early phase) and

53 have been organically developed. These days, W. R. Berkley chooses to prioritise organic growth over acquisitions, mainly because it has the know-how and scale to develop businesses cost-effectively. It also wants to avoid paying the necessary premiums involved in any acquisition. Either way, capital is allocated sparingly and always in a relatively small portion compared to its size. You will not see W. R. Berkley make outlandish acquisitions or big bets on new lines of business.

Flight Centre, a multinational travel agency headquartered in Australia, also shares the same growth philosophy. In my conversation with the CEO and co-founder, he shared the mistakes he had made in the past with acquisitions.[3,4] Such mistakes included buying companies that were unprofitable but which he thought could be turned around, buying companies that had an incongruent cultural philosophy (as integration would not work), and buying companies as a direct route to achieving international expansion. Flight Centre's strategy also steers away from excessively large acquisitions, as this poses risks with integration and the possibility of overpaying. Instead, it focuses on acquiring niche, profitable travel businesses. An example he mentioned was businesses in the luxury wildlife tourism sector—an area requiring deep expertise, making it hard to develop internally but also more attractive to acquire because it was so specialised and fit in well with the business's strategy to expand into niche areas.

Contrast this to the 'bigger is better' approach, where two businesses of similar size come together because one acquires the other. Management teams may be lured by the economies of scale argument, but this often turns out to be a bad use of capital because the larger the acquisition, the greater the risk of cultural and integration problems. Further capital injection is often required following the merger — usually to engage teams of third-party consultants that nut out the details of how the new organisation chart will look. Not only is more capital required, but the management team needs to invest more time to achieve results. Classic examples are the Alcatel and Lucent Technologies merger in 2006 and the Royal Bank of Scotland's acquisition of ABN Amro in 2007.

These were significant bets made by management teams that ultimately did not pay off. In such cases, decision-making can be skewed by a tendency to stay the course, even when new information suggests a change in direction. This is particularly common in mergers and acquisitions, where initial growth assumptions often need revision as due diligence uncovers more details about the companies involved. However, by that point, executives have typically made public commitments to the deal, and under the pressure of market expectations, there is strong momentum to proceed — sometimes even when the facts have changed so drastically that the merger or acquisition no longer makes sense. This is known as *commitment bias*. In the context of flawed decision-making around major acquisitions, management may adjust the business case to justify the deal, often overestimating synergies and underestimating the costs and time required for post-merger integration. I will delve deeper into these group cognitive biases in Chapter 3, but one way to counteract this tendency is to limit the size of acquisitions, thereby containing the potential fallout from commitment biases.

This is exactly what W. R. Berkley does whenever it embarks on any new expansion. It keeps the exposure small, and the business looks for specific niches where it can gain scale and a competitive advantage through many small deals rather than a single large one.

Returning the wealth: Share buybacks and dividends

Once the financial foundations are sufficiently strong, excellent management teams will consider how best to reward investors by returning the wealth that has been accumulated. There are several options at this point:

- **Retain cash.** Accumulating wealth in the company will reflect in a higher share price and capital appreciation for shareholders, though with rising cash balances, there is always great temptation for management teams to spend it on higher salary bills and engage in lavish behaviour.

- **Pay dividends.** The challenge for most management teams is to maintain a consistent and growing dividend over the long term. This requires the underlying business to be stable and growing; many management teams have good intentions when it comes to paying high dividends, but when market cycles go against them, they inevitably slash their dividend as a consequence of shrinking profits.

- **Buying back shares.** History has shown that many executives make poor decisions with share buybacks—many repurchase their own stock at the height of a boom, which depletes shareholder value. Instead, management teams that execute share buybacks when their stock is undervalued deliver the most value back to shareholders.

To illustrate excellent capital allocation decisions when it comes to share buybacks and dividends, W. R. Berkley has paid a cash dividend every year since 1976. Since 2006, it has grown its dividend by 11 per cent per annum[5] and has also repaid US$6.7 billion (57 per cent of its net income) to shareholders via dividends or share buybacks. Consistency and the ability to increase dividends matter.

The power of people allocation

Just like capital, the maximisation of human talent is a skill of strategic allocation that enhances judgement. How do management teams demonstrate high levels of judgement when it comes to people? What directives are executive management giving to teams to ensure the best allocation of people to then drive the best value creation? What clues can we look to as markers for that efficiency in people deployment?

Here is an interesting activity I have seen play out time and time again. If you give managers the LEGO pieces in figure 2-2 and instruct them to make the bridge stable, an overwhelming majority will almost always add an extra piece (either C, D, or E) under piece B to stabilise the structure.

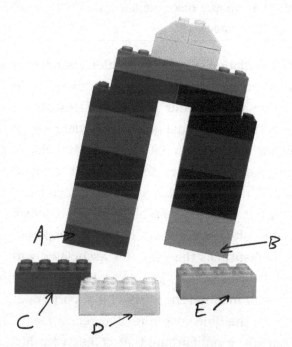

Figure 2-2: How would you stabilise this LEGO bridge?

Nearly zero (or perhaps one or two) managers will take away the existing A block to create the same stabilisation. This is an interesting depiction of the simple psychology embedded within management and teams—when given resources to solve a problem, very few will think to take away existing resources to achieve an outcome; they will almost certainly always add resources. This principle can lead to inefficiencies and ineffectiveness when it comes to allocating investments in people. Many businesses traditionally exercise, with muscle-memory consistency, the practice of throwing people at a problem. This may solve a challenge in the short term; however, for a business to scale and grow profits, smart (perhaps even frugal) people allocation is what drives longevity, and exponential rather than linear profitability. Note: Be careful not to confuse a frugal approach with the unpopular adage of 'doing more with less' by shrinking teams and piling on more work. What you are looking for here is optimised people resource allocation with a demonstrated positive financial impact.

At the very foundation of an organisation's strategy towards its people should be a long-term investment mindset. There should be a belief that valuing your people and ensuring appropriate investment in their individual growth will yield a positive return back to the business. This is not simply about achieving positive employee engagement metrics, though that is a collateral benefit. The reason behind having a long-term approach to employees is simply because it is more profitable to do so. Extensive research highlights the often-overlooked costs of employee attrition, which may well surpass the expenses associated with investing in employee development or providing reasonable salary increases. Not to mention the costs of lost corporate knowledge of the business, the time cost of regular recruitment cycles, and excessive employee onboarding that comes with high attrition.

A typical 'churn and burn' strategy is a costly one that does not allow an organisation to compound its knowledge.

The earlier LEGO analogy offers a simplified view of how to approach people management when tackling a challenge. As organisations reassess their business plans, they must decide whether to add more staff or (the less popular choice) reduce headcount. However, a third, often overlooked option exists beyond adding or subtracting: Organisations can take a strategic approach by regularly evaluating their workforce needs, identifying which roles to retain in-house and which non-essential functions to outsource, and reallocating talent to align with both individual strengths and business priorities. In essence, it is about reconfiguring the entire LEGO bridge to best fit with the pieces at hand.

Outsiders can uncover significant insights into a company's operational strategy by examining annual reports and investor presentations, where investments in technology and systems projects often reveal efforts to enhance internal processes. Such investments indicate that executive teams are embracing innovative approaches to redesign their operating models, reflecting a strategic mindset about workforce allocation. Conversely, unusually high attrition rates can signal a misalignment between role design and the organisation's core strengths, suggesting a need for a thorough review of its operating units.

Looking ahead, the projected decline in the global population, particularly in developed countries, will lead to a shrinking workforce and heightened value of human capital. This demographic shift will compel organisations to operate more efficiently, prioritising technology-led solutions over mere increases in human resources. As technological capabilities advance, enabling smarter and leaner operations, organisations that recognise this trend will cultivate a culture of strategic problem-solving. They will prioritise leveraging technology to optimise their processes, freeing up employees to engage in other crucial tasks that technology cannot replace.

Talent mobility

During a conversation with the management team at Reply SpA, an Italian technology consultancy firm, I discovered a distinctive approach to workforce strategy. Reply competes with much larger rivals by implementing a disaggregated business model and emphasising talent mobility in its workforce strategy. Contrary to expectations, Reply, an agile consultancy, relies primarily on direct employees rather than contractors to meet its resourcing needs (due to the challenging European labour laws regarding contractors). This is what my conversation with management revealed about how effectively Reply has mastered the allocation of people.

Reply's teams are constructed as separate boutique companies, and each company has country-wide exclusivity for their specific market offering. Its management team calls this the 'shopping mall' approach. In 2024, there were roughly 210 different companies within the group. There are intentionally no overlapping offerings within each country, therefore teams never compete at a country level. For example, Italy will have a cyber security team (as a separate company), in addition to a networks team, a data platforms team, and a plethora of other boutique companies that evolve with customer demands. Teams in another country, for example Germany, would mirror the same structure as Italy. This boutique approach is unique in consulting and allows Reply to identify popular market services and replicate the offering in other jurisdictions. Similarly, less popular offerings are dissolved and absorbed. The operating model becomes adaptive to customer trends and creates an automatic feedback loop. The people who lead a successful market offering in a particular country will be the ones who kick-start the same market offering in another country. How Reply allocates people becomes a function of market demand, and employees are incentivised to develop skills in highly sought after areas. It also creates talent mobility as personnel can move within the organisation into business lines and geographies that fit them best. The right personnel are invited to become co-owners of new companies, with a pre-agreed set of buyout terms should the business line reach its growth targets post launch. These built-in mechanisms allow Reply to create mobility in its ranks.

There is also another unique concept that Reply adheres to in its strategic allocation: The management team has embedded in the organisation the concept of maximum margins. When the group's margin reaches a predefined upper limit, this is a signal to encourage its boutique companies to invest and expand further into new industry verticals—to take on more risk. This naturally forces the strategic allocation process to accelerate—people and capital are redeployed into expansion activities that fuel the next phase of company growth. Investments in research and development grow during these phases (innovative niche service offerings are the focus as Reply chooses to compete in under-saturated business lines), and margins naturally fall back down into a target range. It is rare to see management teams define an upper limit on margins, but in Reply's case margins are used as a prompt to strategically reallocate capital and human resources.

Attrition rates and role design

Many employee engagement surveys conducted by organisations show similar themes in terms of what makes an employee stay in their job or, conversely, what would make them leave. A common thread that reappears across all sectors and all organisations when asked about employee motivations for staying in their role, is the opportunity to progress.[6] From an executive management lens, this means an approach to people that encompasses a long-term investment in an individual's future at the company; in other words, an investment in their longevity. This approach is a combination of role design and training which involves building an individual's knowledge, expertise, and capability so they can continue to apply and build knowledge capital for the organisation.

I use the term 'role design' broadly, encompassing not only the responsibilities of a position but also the broader flexibility in professional development opportunities and attention to *how* employees prefer to work. The COVID-19 global pandemic underscored the importance of wide-ranging flexibility in a role—something more critical than we ever imagined. There is a clear correlation between these factors with employee retention.[7,8] Flexibility extends beyond just working hours or the choice between home versus the office; it is about a company supporting individualism, and recognising that a 'one size fits all' approach does not work. Businesses need to support diverse values around flexibility. For some employees, this might even mean allowing the pursuit of a side-hustle, which was previously frowned upon in traditional industries before COVID but is now seen as part of supporting individualism and offering true flexibility.

'Why do we care about employee attrition as external observers?' you might ask. When assessing how well an organisation's leaders have executed a people strategy, an easy marker to look at is tenure and attrition as these are the foundational elements to building people capital in a business. Without stability in teams and the building of organisational knowledge, it becomes harder to deliver on long-term business strategies to generate profits. Low employee tenure and high turnover is likely to indicate something is amiss with role design and therefore resulting in low productivity and erosion of profitability.[9] A clear example of a business that suffers from this challenge is Teleperformance SE, a France-headquartered, global contact centre provider with over 400000 employees. In Europe, Teleperformance provides customer service support for big names like Google, Apple, and Facebook, as well as a number of financial services institutions.[10] Australian clients of Teleperformance include the major telecommunications company, Telstra. Contact centres are generally known to have high turnover in staff due to the monotonous nature of the work; however, Teleperformance is cited to have a turnover rate of 32.9 per cent—well above the average turnover rates for contact centres in Australia, which ranges between 10–25 per cent.[11] Analysis on the cause for this high turnover illustrates that a key contributor is the organisation's unwillingness to support flexible work practices. Position design and accountabilities are difficult to adapt for businesses like contact centres given the repetitive nature of tasks for customer support staff, so other components of role design, such as flexibility, matter even more to ensuring staff retention and minimising attrition.

In Greece, during the COVID-19 pandemic, Teleperformance was slow to adopt working from home practices, giving rise to much employee dissatisfaction and complaint.[10] Much of Teleperformance's questionable behaviour towards its staff during the lockdowns in Greece drew the ire of thousands of its employees, who launched petitions and complaints against the organisation, which reflected in significant drops in its share price. In other words, unhappy employees are bad for business.

CHAPTER 3

Group cognitive biases

The last component in determining a management team's judgement is to ascertain how susceptible to cognitive biases it may be, as it is these biases that pose a risk to the decisions it makes.

For readers familiar with cognitive biases, it is important to highlight what I am referring to here is *group* biases, which are distinctly different to *individual* cognitive biases. In theory, a team of executive managers should make better decisions than individual ones as their skills and experiences complement each other. In practice, however, this is not always true. A group of highly rational and intelligent individuals can still produce sub-optimal outcomes if they become blinded by wider group cognitive biases.

An example of this is the Wells Fargo Scandal of 2016, where senior management at one of the largest banks in the US failed to identify a rampant case of employee fraud in its ranks. Over 5300 employees and managers were sacked for forging customer signatures and opening fake customer accounts in order to meet sales targets. How could one of the largest banks in the US with a stated vision of striving to set 'the standard among the world's great companies for integrity and principled performance' succumb to such rampant criminal behaviour? The failure was due to a multitude of organisational problems, one of which was the CEO's reputation for being non-confrontational and averse to bad news. A subsequent independent report also found that Carrie Tolstedt, the executive in charge of the community banking division (which was at the heart of the fraud), was 'obsessed with control, especially of negative information about the community bank' and was known for maintaining 'an "inner circle" of staff that supported her, reinforced her views, and protected her'.[1] Senior leaders within her division were afraid of airing contrary views.

On paper, the brilliance of Wells Fargo's senior leaders shone — but yet despite all this, a failure of this magnitude was made possible because it was a failure of a group, not of an individual. In this chapter, we explore what causes group cognitive biases, how they can take hold without challenge, and how to identify the signs that group cognitive biases are at work in an organisation.

The causes of group cognitive biases

Almost all of our cognitive biases can be traced back to our Neolithic origins — thousands of years ago, our DNA was hardwired to ensure human survival in harsh and dangerous environments. While much of this programming is no longer necessary today, it endures, much like a computer's operating system running beneath the applications. This ancient coding subtly influences our behaviour, even when we believe we are acting logically or rationally.

We humans are advanced machines, made up of a unique blend of biological hardware and software. Our hardware — our physical bodies — is defined by genetics but can be enhanced through exercise and nutrition. Similarly, our software—our minds—is governed by an underlying operating system, inherited genetically, much like Windows or iOS. Beyond this, we can enhance our minds through education and training, akin to adding new apps or updates. However, while these applications are frequently updated, our operating system evolves at a much slower pace, tied to the physical evolution of our species over generations. Because this evolutionary process is so slow, our operating system has not fully adapted to modern demands, leaving us vulnerable to cognitive errors, especially when we work together in groups.

Let me explain why these group vulnerabilities exist by comparing the development of our operating system in the Neolithic era with its application in today's modern corporate environment.

The gregariousness of human nature

As social beings, we have an innate desire to fit in, leading us to conform in order to collaborate effectively and foster team cohesion. This tendency toward conformity was crucial in our past, aiding our survival, hunting, and group coordination. Naturally, we seek to blend in with others, as we are inherently pack animals rather than solitary creatures.

In the modern corporate world, however, this manifests as members of executive teams becoming 'yes' people, often afraid to question the dominant leaders of the group. In my experience working at one of the world's largest banks, I saw this dynamic first-hand. Senior leaders, simply due to their position within the global hierarchy, were often granted an unchallenged authority. This fostered a culture of excessive deference, where decisions were made based more on rank than reason. Given our social nature, fitting into this hierarchy often meant conforming to this decision-making style, with little room for independent analysis.

The responsibility diffusion effect

Another reason groups are prone to errors in judgement is the perception that decisions made by consensus distribute responsibility across the group, thus diluting individual accountability. The decision made by consensus has a diffused owner. Within smaller groups, the dilution of individual accountability is not material enough to create group cognitive biases. However, as groups become larger—in the case of the corporate world, the size of corporate management teams and boards—the diffusion of individual responsibility is magnified, and the risk of sub-optimal decision-making increases. Groups of highly qualified individuals, who would typically make sound decisions on their own, may therefore make poor choices when acting as a group.

The power of social proof

Because of our innate tendency to seek safety in numbers, we naturally prefer aligning with the majority. This instinct, stemming from our evolutionary past, increased our chances of survival by sticking to the group—whether it was choosing shelter locations or hunting for food, it was always safer to be with than to venture alone. In today's corporate world, we no longer seek physical proximity; instead, we gravitate towards the evidence (the *social proof*) that suggests we are in line with the majority in decision-making situations. Differing from the group can be risky for corporate careers, meaning our independent judgement can be altered by the prevailing views of the majority.

An example of this is from Robert Cialdini's research (popularised in his bestselling book *Influence: The Psychology of Persuasion*) on the effectiveness of encouraging hotel guests to reuse towels in a bid to conserve energy and water. Two appeals were made in the signage for guests. The first was an appeal to the logical brain—messaging that emphasised the environmental benefits of reusing towels; the second was an appeal to conform with the majority of guests—messaging that emphasised the fact that most guests reused their towels. Using social proof as a technique was found to be much more effective than the appeal to logic.

As a former investment banker, a common strategy involved first securing agreements from the most influential stakeholders when raising funds from a consortium of banks or investors. Once these key figures were committed, the others typically followed. In cases of resistance, engaging dissenting bankers in separate negotiations and subsequently presenting them with the terms agreed upon by the majority effectively leveraged social proof to align the entire group. Our decisions, consciously or not, are shaped by the choices of those around us.

Group cognitive biases

A good friend of mine told me a fascinating story about her experience on one of the boards she used to work with. The board was recruiting to fill several director vacancies and had just gone through a thorough interview process with several shortlisted candidates. One of the candidates was a clear front runner; however, a spanner in the works arose when her referee provided a rather unfavourable reference. The referee was an incredibly respected and well-known professional in the industry with significant influence across various networks, though unfortunately also a bit of a bigot. The main problem was that the remarks made by the referee were clearly inappropriate through a professional lens—with repeated emphasis on judgements such as the individual being 'too young' and 'not ready to be a board director', without a substantive basis to support such assertions. The board members were faced with a conundrum: Proceed with the candidate but risk the ire of the bigoted statesman, or take the referee's remarks at face value and reject the otherwise exceptional candidate.

Here is where it gets interesting. The conversation started with board members assuming they would need to reject the candidate—after all, it was a referee she had provided and who had worked with her closely, not to mention that he had a great deal of influence in the industry. To not take his word would most certainly offend him, which was unpalatable from a stakeholder relationship perspective. Conversations then progressed to troubleshooting how the board would let down the candidate and provide the right messaging, as well as selecting an alternative candidate for the appointment. However, then one board member piped up with a different view.

'Don't we think that it's against our values as an organisation and what we stand for, if we were to support statements like that [referring to the referee's comments] by rejecting a preferred candidate who is so well credentialled?'

Mumblings from fellow board members followed.

'I personally feel that those comments and that attitude of the referee is exactly the type of behaviour that we want to shift away from.'

Slowly, nods of support and agreement.

And just like that, the conversation made a full 180 swing the other way, with board members then turning to discussions on how as an organisation it should stand up to the referee, with further talks ensuing on how to have the right conversations to manage him.

This story is revealing on multiple levels, but at its core, it highlights how the direction of a conversation can easily shift with the subtle influence of just one or two individuals. Whether we call it groupthink or a cognitive blindspot, the reality is that human interactions are deeply shaped by individual biases. When left unchecked (as nearly occurred in this case) groupthink can foster a strong, and at times perilous, collective bias.

Now that we have considered the causes of common group errors in judgement, let us explore them further to see which types are most prevalent at the corporate level.

Conformity bias

The stronger this conformity effect, the greater the likelihood that groups will blindly follow the leader and support poor decisions, bypassing a rational assessment of each option. Having served on management teams and boards, I have witnessed first-hand how corporate presentations are often packed with overwhelming amounts of data—numbers, charts, and projections—all designed to steer attendees toward a predetermined decision. These meetings, where the recommendation is typically framed in advance, often become little more than box-ticking exercises. While a more open forum that encourages questioning assumptions and exploring different perspectives would be more conducive to making the best decision, the sheer volume of information presented often creates social pressure to avoid being the dissenting voice. After all, who wants to be seen as difficult? This is where the pressure to conform takes hold.

Another tactic often employed by corporate executives to achieve their desired outcome is *front running*, where pre-emptive discussions are initiated with key influencers on an individual basis—ideas are sounded out and proposed with the purpose being to win over the key influencers one by one. If enough prior consensus is gained, the driver of the decision can win the group over even before an opportunity for open debate. It also becomes extremely difficult to veto a decision when it already has the support of the majority, so the outliers of this front-running tactic are left to conform with the group decision—they are experiencing *conformity bias*.

Avoidance bias

Large teams gravitate towards the most risk-averse decision because it feels like the safest choice. I have been in many meetings where positive ideas gain momentum, only to be derailed by a single voice highlighting potential risks (usually reputational risks, personal liability, or other issues that could often be mitigated). Gradually, as if the vitality of the idea is balanced on a precarious see-saw, risk-aversion starts to spread through the group. The merits of the idea waver, and ultimately, the group settles on the lowest common denominator, causing momentum to stall. Aversion is a powerful emotion, and even the original supporters of the idea may hesitate to push forward once a conservative stance has been introduced. No one wants to be the one who ignored the risks and went ahead anyway, as this could harm their reputation, not to mention the company's. The outcome is a group bias (avoidance bias) towards the most risk-averse view, skewing the decision-making process by placing too much emphasis on risk and not enough on potential benefits.

The avoidance bias is magnified in a group environment, but it is a phenomenon that exists within all individuals because of our inherent loss aversion. The psychologists Daniel Kahneman and

Amos Tversky, in their study 'Prospect theory: An analysis of decision under risk',[2] found that individuals presented with the choice between a 50 per cent chance of winning $100, or the option to take a guaranteed $50, almost always chose the guaranteed $50. The theory is that individuals feel the emotional pain of loss much more than the pleasure of winning. This effect is magnified in a team environment and if left imbalanced, this avoidance bias can skew decision-making towards inaction and risk minimisation rather than exploration and calculated risk-taking.

Social loafing

Also known as bystander apathy, *social loafing* occurs when personal accountability diminishes within a group. This phenomenon was famously demonstrated in the early 20th century by engineer Maximilien Ringelmann, who conducted an experiment where participants were asked to pull on a rope, first individually and then as part of a group. The results revealed that individuals exerted much more effort when pulling alone compared to when pulling as a group, with effort decreasing as group size increased. This experiment highlighted how, in group settings, individuals tend to diffuse their efforts when responsibility is shared.

In the corporate world, social loafing can arise when there are significant delegations of authority. Critical issues may be overlooked when everyone assumes someone else will take responsibility, particularly when authority has been distributed. Similarly, management teams that heavily rely on third-party consultants can obscure their own responsibilities by outsourcing decision-making. Because consultants often lack the deep understanding and context of the company, over-reliance on their advice can lead to short-sighted and poorly thought-out decisions.

The well-known Public Goods Game illustrates this psychological principle. Similar to the Prisoner's Dilemma experiment, a group functions well when all members contribute fairly to a common pool that benefits everyone. However, when some members contribute less but continue to receive equal benefits, others notice and begin to reduce their contributions as well. The impact of social loafing in this experiment leads to a breakdown in collaboration, shifting the group from team players to self-interested individuals.

Status quo bias

When organisations become entrenched in their routines, management teams often resist disrupting established strategies, even when faced with changing market conditions or new information. This resistance is rooted in *status quo bias*, where teams are reluctant to initiate change due to fear of potential negative consequences. As a result, adapting and realigning priorities becomes challenging, and the group tends to default to familiar, safe decisions.

Once status quo bias takes hold, and especially when combined with conformity bias, the organisation can develop a strong resistance to change. The fear of venturing into new areas or taking risks can cause the company to stagnate, preferring to follow its peers rather than innovate. While key decision-makers may believe they are steering the company cautiously, they often overlook the larger risk: missed opportunities that could eventually disrupt their existing business models and threaten the company's long-term success. By clinging to the familiar, the organisation may inadvertently expose itself to greater dangers than the perceived risks of change.

Availability bias

Our inclination to make decisions based on readily available information is a mental shortcut that helps us process information quickly and efficiently. However, this can lead us to mistakenly prioritise what is most immediate or memorable over more relevant facts that deserve consideration. In executive team meetings, decision-making hinges on the collective judgement and expertise each member brings. The CEO depends on the financial insights of the Chief Financial Officer, the operational knowledge of the Chief Operating Officer, and the market expertise of the Chief Strategy Officer. *Availability bias* occurs when the team places too much reliance on the information presented, assuming it accurately reflects the most critical facts within each executive's domain.

A stark example of this is the Wells Fargo scandal, where the information provided to the broader executive team was not reflective of the actual issues within the division. Yet, due to availability bias, this incomplete or misleading information became the primary basis for decision-making, ultimately contributing to the crisis.

In my role as an investor, I engaged in exploratory discussions with a publicly listed Polish company whose primary product was a chat software program designed to help companies interact more efficiently with customers. The software product would be heavily impacted by the release of ChatGPT and the broader wave of generative artificial intelligence (AI) that was forthcoming. The company had no alternative but to embrace the use of large language models and generative AI—if it did not, the company's customers would leave for new AI software products. The management team agreed it needed to adopt AI, but the question was how. In my discussions, the team pointed to a key decision that was being considered internally to evolve the business—the choice for the company to develop its own large language model given the abundance of chat data it already had, or to integrate and modify off-the-shelf large language models as a faster (but more costly) approach. This decision was not an easy one to make. The technological requirements and implications associated with each option would be familiar to the Chief Technology Officer, but other variables such as the impact to customer churn and competitor alternatives would be the realm of the CEO and Chief Operating Officer.

To make a decision as important as this one, each executive needs to cover their own area of expertise, so they rely on the information from others when making a team decision. A natural mental shortcut is to assume that everyone in the group has disseminated complete information, when in fact the body of information may be missing a crucial element. If the Chief Technology Officer makes a recommendation based on current technological constraints, the CEO and Chief Operating Officer understandably assume that the recommendation is based on complete information and use this to make a judgement call—when in fact, better opportunities might come up in future. In other words, managers rely on the expertise of their peers when they make decisions as a group.

Ultimately, the company chose to implement external large language models immediately while simultaneously developing their own, which would first be beta tested by its internal teams. From an outsider's perspective, this is a forward-thinking strategy, especially given that generative AI is still in its infancy; its full potential remains to be seen. By adopting external models, the company can quickly adapt to current AI developments while allowing itself time to build proprietary models for future use. Although using external models involves higher costs in the short term, concurrently developing in-house models offers greater long-term cost efficiency and flexibility for integration across the company's products. This approach enables management to remain agile and adaptable, balancing the immediate need for AI adoption with the flexibility required for future advancements in generative AI.

Commitment bias

In Chapter 2, I explored how management teams can become locked into a decision, unable to pivot even when the facts urge otherwise. Often, this happens after a public commitment to a particular strategy, where the weight of expectations from investors, the media, and internal stakeholders pressures them to stay the course—despite growing evidence that it is a misstep. This phenomenon, known as *commitment bias*, is a cognitive bias that affects individuals, but in group settings, it is compounded by conformity bias and status quo bias, creating an even stronger inertia that resists change.

This bias can manifest in various ways. A notable example is a US financial services company I encountered, which embarked on the ambitious migration of its customer transaction management system to a new start-up provider that promised faster, more accurate, and transparent record-keeping through innovative blockchain technology. The financial services company was cautious about the move—knowing the high risk and substantial work involved—particularly since blockchain adoption in the industry was still rare, and the service provider was a company in its infancy. After months of management presentations and debates, the leadership team decided to take the plunge, viewing the transition as an opportunity to be market-leading, with the potential rewards outweighing the risks.

The deal was announced with great fanfare, stirring curiosity from market observers. But a year later, the blockchain technology had failed to meet expectations. The migration remained ongoing, and unforeseen complexities had diluted the anticipated benefits. Despite mounting challenges and the evident limitations of the technology, the management team at the financial services company remained committed to its decision, bound by the promises it had publicly championed and the pressure to deliver on its strategic overhaul.

This is a textbook example of group commitment bias, where a company, like a speeding train, stays on its set tracks, unable to change course even as the facts cry out for a different direction. The story serves as a reminder of how difficult it can be to reverse course when momentum, reputation, and groupthink are in play—an all-too-common trap for even the most capable leader.

Indicators of group cognitive biases

Insiders, such as board directors or management teams, can identify group cognitive biases more efficiently given their intimate knowledge of internal information and their familiarity with the relationship dynamics within the management team. Outsiders may not be privy to this information, but they can still use observable information to make an educated assessment of the strengths and weaknesses of an executive group.

Human beings and relationships are dynamic, so the objective is not to pinpoint the precise issues within a team, but rather to determine a reasonable range of outcomes through logical deduction based on observable facts. Thinking back to the Judgement Equation, we are making an informed decision on the likely impairment to a team's judgement score, based on such observable data.

The question becomes: How can someone external to a management team identify whether group cognitive biases are at work within the team?

Crossover backgrounds

To combat conformity bias, observe the background and skills of a business's senior leaders. Older organisations have a tendency to accumulate senior leaders who have been promoted through the internal ranks. If all the senior leaders are internally sourced, the views and mindset of the group will be tainted by how things have been done in the past, not necessarily what is required for the future.

Senior leaders who have crossed over from different career paths should be seen favourably—they possess the knowledge of several business languages and have been exposed to different viewpoints. For instance, senior leaders who have crossed over from a legal background into operations can be more effective at negotiating terms with suppliers and can more effectively assess risks while balancing the commercial objectives of the business. Crossovers can be achieved not only by welcoming varied skill sets, but also by welcoming leaders from other industries into the team. A marketing executive can offer a fresh perspective if they come from a marketing agency or competitor.

Given the transparency of information available today, it is a simple task to determine the number of executives that have crossover backgrounds. To minimise conformity bias, a healthy mix between loyal company servants and leaders with crossover backgrounds will provide a fresh perspective while paying heed to the foundational strengths of the business.

An interesting example is the Coca-Cola Company. Today its website lists 40 senior executives. An outsider can make reasonable logical deductions about the company as a result of the sheer number of people within this executive group. We can assume there will be a high degree of cognitive bias. We can also imagine a slow-moving, government-like decision-making engine that will err on the side of risk-averse choices (avoidance bias)—taking calculated risks would be very unlikely.

There is a strong argument to question whether the Chair and CEO would have direct regular contact with each of the other 39 executives; the more likely scenario is that there is a sub-hierarchy within the senior leadership team. The following executives are listed as the top seven:

- Chair and Chief Executive Officer

- President and Chief Financial Officer

- Executive Vice President and Global Chief Marketing Officer

- Senior Vice President and Treasurer, Head of Corporate Finance

- Senior Vice President and Chief Information Security Officer

- Executive Vice President and President, International Development

- President, Global Category—Coca-Cola.

Even with an outside understanding of the nature of the Coca-Cola Company's business, we can surmise these top seven executives have critical portfolios that form a large proportion of the overall decision-making remit of the organisation. By delving deeper, we can also see the respective years in which these executives joined the Coca-Cola Company: 1996, 1988, 1995, 2006, 2020, 1996, 2004. The skew is towards those that have significant internal experience. While this can prove beneficial for the retention of cultural history, outsiders can also deduce that decision-making will likely skew towards repeating what has already been done in the past. A challenge to the status quo is very unlikely.

Size of executive team

The number of key decision-makers in an executive group provides a great insight into how the organisation is partitioned and the dynamics of the decision-making process. In my experience, the size of the senior group should be no larger than five to eight people (including the CEO), depending on the type of organisation and how many divisions it has. These theoretical limits factor in the ability of the CEO to maintain meaningful relationships with four to seven direct reports—any more than this and it can be reasonably assumed that the team is too large for any one person to regularly meet with each member and effectively manage them. In addition, as the number of key decision-makers begins to exceed these bounds, the effect of social loafing and status quo bias seep in—each member's contribution to the decision-making process will diminish if clear lines of accountability and responsibility are not defined. Moreover, the ability for the management team to effect change is hampered with each further decision-maker added to the group.

A scan of the Ernst & Young (EY) global executive committee can explain why its plan to split its audit and consulting businesses failed in 2023. All up, EY listed 17 executives as global leaders on its website in 2024. These 17 individuals are split by sub-teams: Global Executive, Functions, Service Lines, Geographies, and Committees. Already an outsider can see the potential for confusion regarding how these sub-teams are delineated. For example, there is significant crossover between Geographies, Service Lines, and Functions. The decision to split EY's core businesses would have been a game changer for the organisation; however, it is unsurprising that the plan failed and the status quo prevailed.

Some readers may wonder given the sheer volume of people employed by EY how it could shrink its major decision-makers to five to eight from 17. The key, which we will cover in Part 3, is to create an organisational structure akin to a centralised conglomerate and therefore split out new entities, which will run themselves with their own executive leadership teams. Despite being many times the size of EY, Berkshire Hathaway has kept a notoriously lean executive team of decision-makers.

Another lesser-known centralised conglomerate is Vitec Software from Sweden. This company has effectively streamlined its decision-making process by limiting the number of key decision-makers. Its subsidiaries function within a hub-and-spoke model centred around the head office, giving each subsidiary the autonomy and responsibility to make key decisions within a broadly defined materiality threshold. This approach empowers the executive leaders of each subsidiary and distributes decision-making authority, thereby avoiding the typical corporate structure that relies on large group decision-making and the cognitive biases that often accompany it. Keeping the number of key decision-makers lean is central to minimising the risk of groupthink and other blindspots that can develop within a large group.

Clear accountability

When the responsibilities and accountabilities of executive managers become blurred, the risk of social loafing increases. When it is unclear who is responsible, it is human nature to wait and see who will take the lead. The remedy for social loafing is to ensure that the remit of each executive is clear and does not overlap.

Taking Salesforce as an example, while it has a relatively large senior management team of 13, each executive does have a defined remit. Here is a list of Salesforce's C-suite executive titles in 2024:

- CEO

- Chief Technology Officer

- Chief Financial Officer

- Chief Marketing Officer

- Chief Operating Officer

- Chief Product Officer

- Chief Information Officer

- Chief Business Officer / Chief of Staff

- Chief Revenue Officer

- Chief People Officer

- Chief Legal Officer

- Chief Engineering Officer

- Chief Impact Officer.

Even as outsiders peering into the company, we can see where potential weaknesses may lie. The Chief Business Officer / Chief of Staff overlaps with several other executives, in particular the Chief Operating Officer. We can surmise the main role of this executive is to relay key messages from the CEO, but this is a double-up and the role does not have its own clear portfolio carved out. Ideally, the CEO takes full accountability of managing the executive team; however, in this example we can make a reasonable assumption that he has outsourced components of the role to the Chief Business Officer / Chief of Staff.

Delving deeper into the history of Salesforce, we can see that the CEO has expressed the intention to wind back his responsibilities for a few years. In August 2018, he appointed a Co-CEO, a move which did not work out well (the Co-CEO left after a short 18-month stint). With this additional context, we can deduce that the role of Chief Business Officer / Chief of Staff may be a second attempt at allowing the CEO to wind back his duties.

The Co-CEO model has been shown to go against the principle of minimising cognitive biases. This approach has been proven unsuccessful by companies such as SAP (the Co-CEO lasted six months) and Oracle (the company reverted back to a sole CEO after five years). Companies that pursue this approach unnecessarily magnify the degree of difficulty with which they choose to run their company.

Back to Salesforce's executive team, the Chief Impact Officer role also appears out of place as their remit covers all aspects of the business, which we can expect to overlap with the responsibilities of other executives. There has been a trend in recent times to emphasise the strength of corporate citizenship (in the areas of environmental, social, and governance, or ESG) through the promotion of a Chief Impact Officer to champion sustainability.

The separation of this accountability naturally diminishes the focus of the other executives in this area. We can imagine the Chief Impact Officer having to work closely with other executives to embed sustainability across the organisation, when an alternative approach could be to set sustainability objectives for each executive.

Looking through the rest of the executive team, we can see accountabilities have been allocated according to technical expertise—marketing, legal, technology, financial, people, and engineering—which is a logical way of assigning accountabilities based on the technical requirements of the business (and the core skills of each executive) and is also a positive step towards avoiding social loafing.

It is often better to have a smaller executive team; each individual needs to have a sufficiently differentiated accountability otherwise the risk of social loafing grows. Other than the exceptions highlighted, Salesforce has clean lines of accountability for the most part.

Executive management tenure and turnover

There is no doubt a management team's experience with a company is critical for retaining and continuing corporate knowledge. It is an asset that enables a company to remember its history and context so past mistakes are not repeated in future decisions. The longer the tenure of the team, the more extensive the knowledge base. There is, however, a caveat: Small degrees of turnover within a management team does come with some benefits. By changing a small portion of the team intermittently, the group is able to bring in fresh perspectives and stave off the effects of groupthink and status quo bias. Just like any top-performing sporting team at its peak, new talent is blooded in small doses to give opportunity to infuse new skill and ensure a healthy level of questioning of the status quo.

PART I: RECAP

How good is management's judgement?

♦ Judgement comes from an observable foundation of:

$$\text{Judgement} = \frac{\text{Decision Accuracy} + \text{Strategic Allocation}}{\text{Group Cognitive Biases}}$$

♦ Even outsiders can determine a management team's decision accuracy. Look at the previous strategic plans outlined in its reporting — has it demonstrated a track record of success in overcoming challenges?

♦ If earnings are growing and financial results are consistently positive, it is likely the right decisions are being made — it is also likely that the company is winning market share.

♦ Financial results take many quarters to be realised — in the meantime, look for signs that progress is being made: Have new expansion plans begun? Have new distribution agreements been signed? Have new products been launched?

♦ Look for Net Promoter Scores and employee satisfaction scores — satisfied internal and external stakeholders are a sign that a management team has made the right 'people' decisions.

♦ Of equal importance, though often overlooked, are employee attrition rates. Consistently high attrition rates indicate a loss of corporate knowledge and diminish the company's ability to effectively reallocate talent and compound knowledge.

- Management teams that squeeze every dollar now will face a future where there is no more juice left — look for companies that pursue harder long-term decisions and are prepared to give up some of the short-term upside.

- Cost-cutting management teams do not grow businesses — they most likely have poor judgement.

- Management teams that constantly benchmark against their peers end up being trend-followers and not trend-setters. The only worthwhile benchmarking involves monitoring societal trends and evolving with customer preferences.

- The strategic allocation of capital and people are hidden multipliers that enhance a management team's judgement score. Never underestimate the benefit both capital and people can give to a management team's tool chest.

- Look for companies that solve problems through the use of technology and by adapting their operations, rather than throwing people at the issue.

- Look for companies that use capital wisely, investing in small bolt-on acquisitions rather than big bets — multiple, smaller acquisitions in niche areas is always more favourable than one large acquisition.

- Companies that demonstrate the ability to build a growing cash balance over the long term are more likely to spend it wisely.

- Share buybacks are best conducted when share prices are undervalued. Adept management teams demonstrate the ability to pick when their stock is under- or overvalued.

- Steady debt levels are a sign the management team recognises the hidden time cost of excessive and wanton use of debt.

- If you cannot easily delineate the roles and responsibilities in an executive team based on each title, chances are that the executives themselves may not be able to either.

- A good size for an executive management team is five to eight people. Beware of large executive management teams — they will be impaired by slow and bureaucratic decision-making processes and are likely to include some members who do not add great value.

- Executives with experience in diverse fields provide a fresh perspective that challenges the inherent tendency towards conformity.

- Just like a good sporting team, good management teams have a good mix of company veterans and newcomers who bring external perspectives.

PART II
Alignment

'Fine art is that in which the hand, the head,
and the heart of man go together.'

— **John Ruskin**

Warren Buffett famously remarked, 'Price is what you pay. Value is what you get,' a distinction that resonates beyond the stock market and applies aptly to executive teams. Exceptional leadership should, in theory, translate into company growth, with executive compensation being the price paid by owners. Ideally, higher pay should correspond with improved performance, yet this is not always the case. Much like in financial markets, inefficiencies abound—many well-paid executives fail to deliver meaningful results, while others drive substantial value without commanding exorbitant salaries or being hailed as 'rockstar' leaders. What, then, accounts for this discrepancy, and how can boards and owners optimise the value generated by their executive teams?

In this part, we explore the second pillar of the Founder Framework: alignment. Great management teams are driven by the right motivations. Personal ambitions align with the long-term best interests of the company and its owners. The corporate world often focuses on financial incentives to drive motivation, but this approach alone is limited and does not fully account for the complexity of human psychological drivers. *Self-determination theory*, a psychological framework developed by Edward L Deci and Richard M Ryan,[1] offers a comprehensive understanding of human motivation, which is key to explaining effective executive management alignment. Essentially, motivation consists of both intrinsic and extrinsic factors. Intrinsic motivators are internal drivers and emotions that fuel self-motivation, offering satisfaction from within through interest, enjoyment, curiosity, and personal values, without the need for external rewards. Extrinsic motivators, on the other hand, are rewards derived from external sources, such as financial incentives, recognition, and ego. Based on this it comes as no surprise that financial incentives represent only one form of extrinsic motivators and therefore only a small portion of what drives us.

On a deeper psychological level, an over-reliance on extrinsic rewards can actually weaken intrinsic motivation.[2] In other words, the excessive use of financial incentives may unintentionally undermine authentic executive drive. *Cognitive evaluation theory* sheds light on this dynamic, with evidence showing that an overemphasis on external rewards can erode intrinsic motivation, limit autonomy, and shift focus from the task's inherent value to the pursuit of the reward itself. In more extreme cases, such incentives may even be viewed negatively, as individuals feel that rewards are being dangled conditionally, reducing their sense of self-control. This pressure can strip the work of its intrinsic satisfaction, leading to a gradual decline in both motivation and engagement over time.

To be clear, extrinsic motivators like rewards and incentives are not inherently harmful. However, their use must be thoughtfully balanced with intrinsic drivers, as they can, if misapplied, undermine the very motivation they seek to enhance.

Shareholders and board directors constantly undervalue the power of intrinsic motivators because they are difficult to define and report on. Yet, we see time and time again that it is not enough to be the most talented team. The team that remains the most motivated (not necessarily the best remunerated) is the one that wins.

In my experience as an investor, I have often seen executives place greater emphasis on short- to medium-term performance metrics at the expense of long-term business sustainability. This focus can complicate the pursuit of true alignment. Consider an organisation's strategic plan, typically spanning three to five years, alongside annual business plans that detail specific actions and targets. The challenge lies in discerning long-term alignment within a management team that is primarily driven by these shorter-term frameworks. One effective approach is to carefully examine the strategic plans for consistency over time. Since management not only crafts but is also accountable for executing these plans, any indications of long-term vision woven into the initiatives can offer valuable insight.

A more comprehensive method, however, is to examine the deeper extrinsic and intrinsic motivators that drive the management team. On the extrinsic side, incentives—whether financial, such as performance bonuses, or non-financial, such as industry recognition—are clear motivators. Yet, understanding the intrinsic motivators—the values, passions, beliefs, and aspirations that management holds—can reveal a deeper, more enduring commitment to the organisation's success. It is essential, though, to avoid the misconception that intrinsic motivators alone are superior. While they are indeed powerful, the most effective alignment is achieved through a balanced combination of both intrinsic and extrinsic motivators. This synergy can unlock what is often the most valuable form of alignment: psychological ownership, an organisation's 'hidden superpower'.

Psychological ownership is the deep, inherent sense of personal investment in a business,[3] even in the absence of legal ownership, that inspires founder-like behaviours. This is the hidden superpower in achieving optimal alignment. By effectively balancing both extrinsic and intrinsic motivators within an organisation, the ultimate goal is to cultivate an executive team whose actions are driven by this powerful sense of psychological ownership. Shareholders ultimately want the stewards of their company to think and behave like them—like owners. This requires a feeling of possessiveness and being psychologically tied to an organisation—a sense that the company *belongs* to the executive team, which is a cognitive-affective state in which a deep sense of ownership is developed as a product of the management team's hard work and labour.[4] The management team becomes motivated by the same goals as the owners of the company, achieving one of the three traits of a great management team.

This formidable superpower serves as a vital measure for evaluating alignment, offering deep insights into a company's potential for success. In chapters 4 and 5, we explore the essential extrinsic and intrinsic motivators and how, when artfully balanced, they unlock the often-underestimated force of psychological ownership. We examine how external observers can assess the alignment between management teams and an organisation's objectives.

To truly illustrate the transformative power of alignment, let me share the compelling story of a founder whose remarkable success was driven by this psychological force.

Driven by passion[5]

This is the story of how a multi-billion-dollar company got started. It's 1935, and a bright-eyed young man has just graduated with a Bachelor of Arts degree in commerce and business from university. Still under British control, Hong Kong is small, but the densely populated island is his home. He'd only moved there five years before to follow in the footsteps of his father's employment, having originally hailed from Guangdong, the southern Chinese province bordering Hong Kong. His dream was to study civil engineering in China; how he ended up graduating with a BA degree in commerce and business in Hong Kong is only a circumstance of his family's financial situation. The course had been funded by his father's employer. As with all things, there were no free lunches — the benefactor was a real estate firm that embedded the expectation that the young man would join the firm's ranks after his graduation. The young man had no complaints. It was a good deal. Compelling enough to motivate him to pursue business over engineering. His family would welcome saving money on university fees, and the role would offer him a stable start to his career.

In 1935, Hong Kong was only one of the few free ports in the world. It had inherited the social structures of the British and, being a trading hub, it was able to weather the Great Depression much better than its neighbours. As a central trade hub between the East and West, Hong Kong was supplied with an abundance of domestic and international labour, as well as supplies essential to building the infrastructure of a growing city. Although Hong Kong itself was on the fast track to prosperity, its original motherland, China, still reeling from the economic disruptions caused by the Great Depression a few years earlier, was brought further to its knees only a couple of years later with the eruption of an internal civil war. To make matters worse, the Japanese invaded China in 1937. The combination of these circumstances led to an increasing influx of mainland migrants into Hong Kong, with the less fortunate wayfarers ending up in refugee camps within Hong Kong.

Against this backdrop, no one could blame the young man for taking the safe choice and choosing to join the firm that funded his degree upon graduation. It guaranteed him a safe salaried life in the growing property sector in an economically stable city. Besides, there were perks such as business trips to China, which were unheard of at the time. It was a perfectly safe path trodden by many before him.

It was on one of these business trips to Shanghai that he would attend a seminar from which an early idea would be sowed, one that would lead him to give up his salaried career and instead take the untrodden path in life: the life of a founder. His dreams to become a civil engineer would not be fulfilled, but the young man knew little of the fact his attendance at this seminar would lead him down the path of founding a multi-billion-dollar global business. One totally unrelated to the real estate sector, one he would eventually hand over to his not-yet-born son, one that would be listed on the stock market, and one that his family would remain the majority shareholder of 80 years later.

The talk was called 'Soya beans: The cow of China'. The topic was totally unrelated to his line of work, but something called out to the young man. The speaker was an American by the name of Julean Arnold, a diplomat who had spent decades posted in Nanking and was well-versed with Chinese history. In his presentation, Julean argued the nutritional benefits of soybeans. He went on to proclaim the plant's indispensable role in preserving the health of the population of China, which would otherwise have fallen victim to mass malnourishment owing to the scarcity of meat in the country and the perpetual food shortfall resulting from its burgeoning population. It was the humble soybean, so he declared, that was the unsung hero of China. It was the soybean that had sustained the protein needs of the population for centuries. The unassuming legume was relatively easy to farm and did not require the same resource intensity of meat-based proteins. Being a well-known ingredient in Chinese diets, the assertion was plausible, but it was far from accepted fact. But to the young man, whether soybeans single-handedly prevented the starvation of the Chinese population or not was an irrelevant question. What mattered was the undisputed nutritional benefit of this well-known plant. That was the thought he took back to Hong Kong as a 27-year-old.

By 1939, the civil war in China and the Japanese invasion had led to a surge in refugees seeking shelter in the relative safety of Hong Kong. It was in this imperfect economic soil that the seed of a new corporate behemoth was sown.

Some say fortune favours the brave. But in this case, it wasn't bravery that rewarded the young man. It was a combination of curiosity and memory. It was curiosity that first led him to volunteer at a newly opened refugee camp. His curiosity quickly led to concern as he saw first-hand the agony of war. He witnessed severely malnourished refugees suffering from vitamin deficiencies resulting from the disruption of food supplies and destruction of wealth. He wished he could help — and this was where his memory kicked in. He already knew the solution. It had been planted in his mind at the seminar he had attended two years prior. That was where he had heard about all the nutritional benefits of the soybean milk and how it could replace cow's milk and beef at a fraction of the cost.

He did not have the financial means to feed all the refugees by himself. And although soya bean milk had been a well-known feature of Chinese diets for thousands of years, he did not know much about the topic. So how did a young man of 20-something come to solve this problem?

The answer to this story draws parallels to many other successful businesses. The founding of solid businesses is rarely based on perfectly articulated business plans executed in giant leaps — instead, they arise incrementally through a simmering stew of ideas and a practical need to solve real-life problems. And this case was no different. Oftentimes as outsiders, we see only the end result of the hugely successful multinational company, not the series of imperfect experiments that bubble underneath — a path of natural evolution leading to eventual success. To the young man, the aim wasn't to feed all the refugees all at once in one heroic bound. He realised the key was to break down the problem. Overall success would be achieved if he could resolve each part of the problem, one step at a time.

The problem was the need to affordably and efficiently feed all the malnourished refugees in Hong Kong. But first he needed to be sure if he could solve the problem for just one refugee camp. Together with his fellow group of volunteers, the young man bought some soybeans, brown sugar, a grinder, a kettle, and some cheesecloth with the hopes that they could help nourish just one small group of people. At this stage he had no grand plans — it was simply an experiment he was trying to make work. They set up a stall within the camp and taught refugees how to make soybean milk for themselves. There was enough for one bowl of soybean milk for each refugee per day. He had taken the first step.

It was unclear whether the experiment would fail or succeed, but given the plight of the refugees, it was a risk that had to be taken. The initial financial outlay was minimal, and the risk was further split between the group of volunteers. Besides, there was always the ability to stop the experiment at any time. In other words, he had made a calculated bet where the risk-reward scenario was in his favour. The potential loss was limited but the rewards were uncapped. It didn't take long before he knew the answer to his experiment. The health of the refugees had drastically improved over the course of one month thanks to the self-administered bowl-a-day prescription of soybean milk.

The success of the experiment fuelled the young man's dreams and shone an internal light on a greater purpose behind his dreams. He had proven he could help this group of refugees, and he wanted to help more. Beyond that, he dreamed of building a business that would make this nutritious drink available to the entire population of Hong Kong. If he could make this work so successfully on such a small scale, why couldn't he buy more grinders, kettles, and cheesecloths and simply multiply the output? Given the abundance of soybeans and the simplicity of the production process, soybean milk would be much cheaper for consumers and offer just as much nutrition as cow's milk. It excited him further to see the compelling case for consumers — he visualised it being sold as a replacement for cow's milk, at a much lower price.

Having sought and gained the support of Hong Kong's new Director of Medical Services (an open-minded doctor who had spent significant time overseas) and with the newfound gravitas that came with this support, the young man received the final nudge he needed to bring his dream to life. Unlike the initial experiment, the pursuit of this dream would require all his focus and energy. He quit his job in real estate and managed to secure HK$15 000 from a group of four friends who had taken an interest in his quirky soybean milk formulations. The initial capital was enough for him to launch The Hong Kong Soya Bean Products Company (HKSBP) in 1939. There was no machinery designed for large-scale production of soybean milk at the time, so the founding group had to design its own equipment by modifying imported industrial equipment. It was a simple factory, with a layout based on a dairy factory.

The product was to be called Vita Milk, a soybean milk concoction infused with additional calcium, cod liver oil, and vitamins. It would be sold at HK$0.06 in half-pint glass bottles. Even with the enthusiasm of all involved, the total demand from customers on the first day of operations amounted to a grand total of nine bottles. In that moment, the young man realised that experiments are one thing but growing a business enterprise would be an entirely different beast.

The first few years would prove to be extremely challenging, mainly because the nutritional evidence that the business's marketing campaign hinged upon was not well received by consumers. China's people were well accustomed to the use of soybeans; in fact, for thousands of years, ingredients such as soy sauce, tofu and bean curd had been staples of Chinese cuisine. But for some reason, as the young man discovered, even a well-reasoned marketing plan can fall prey to human nature's inherent apprehension about trying new products. An unfounded public perception arose that suggested soybeans, when cooked and eaten in a 'normal' fashion, were totally healthy to the human diet, and yet if the same ingredient was crushed, its resultant juice would lead to a whole range of ailments such as diarrhoea, indigestion, and stomach aches.

It did not matter that the public perception was unsubstantiated and incorrect. Our founder realised that over the short term, consumer sentiment tends to be dictated by irrationalities. The introduction of new products often involves significant lead times and requires perseverance to push through the initial barriers to achieve consumer acceptance. It is only over the long term that the consumer will eventually be wooed.

The young man was ready to play the long game. He was young. This was his business — he would will it into success. The incentives and motivation were there, but he soon discovered there were many more formidable obstacles to overcome before Vita Milk was to be widely accepted by the public.

The most important element of the product was not right at the beginning. The taste. It simply did not taste very good. Consumers were turned off because of the strong beany flavour and the bitter aftertaste. The product, even by the young man's own admission, 'had a lot to be desired'. And then there was another issue. The product spoiled quickly, even faster than cow's milk. The initial approach was to model the product on cow's milk, adopting the same industry standard of a half-pint milk bottle with paper cap and hood. He quickly realised that the rules of preserving cow's milk did not apply to soybean milk. On the worst days, the rate at which the milk soured was so great that it cancelled out the number of new bottles being manufactured.

The young man was determined to overcome these serious issues. Instead of wallowing over the overwhelming problems at hand, he decided to break each hurdle down into discrete, attainable portions — in much the same way he had viewed helping the refugees in the first place.

The first issue was taste. His experiment with the refugees had proven to be nutritionally successful, but it was not a true test of taste. They were drinking Vita Milk out of nutritional necessity, not because they gravitated towards the taste. Nutrition alone was not an irresistible selling point. He needed consumers to crave the product. That was the end goal, but he also knew that taste was subjective to each consumer. What may be delicious for some could be mediocre for others. It depended on outside factors beyond his control. For instance, cultural upbringing often dictates food and taste preferences. The tolerance for some flavours may be more widely accepted by people who have experienced the sensation previously — for example, spice is an acquired taste that people will have differing sensitivities to. How could he create a ubiquitous taste that would appeal broadly?

To capture the taste buds of the masses, he first needed to find his community of customers. Who would be Vita Milk's first loyal supporters? If he could capture their tastebuds, he stood a chance of eventually learning enough from them to capture the rest of the market. So again, he broke down the problem into a smaller experiment where the risk-to-reward ratio was in his favour. Then the idea hit him suddenly. Who had a need for nutrition, yet could give him a platform to continue testing the product? Children. Their taste buds were untainted and there would be no shortage of honest opinions. Schools would be the ready-made focus groups he needed to create his own platform for the experiment.

The young man recalled reading about an American scholar by the name of Yan Tze Chiu who had written a PhD thesis at Cornell University. The thesis discussed improvements to the production process of making soybean milk. Dr Chiu was highly regarded by the Hong Kong government, having previously published similar research in the region. He would be the perfect partner to collaborate with. The feeling was mutual, as Dr Chiu was excited to be approached by a business that could put into practice much of his research. And so the young man began working with Dr Chiu, with the goal of convincing the government to supply schools with Vita Milk. The academic would be the spokesperson for the nutritional benefits of soybean milk, and tasting sessions would be held as a demonstration that nutrition did not have to come at the cost of taste. The more sessions they conducted, the more adjustments the young man could make to improve the taste. He learned it was rare to strike perfection with the first attempt in business; rather, it was much like tuning a fine guitar. It required small adjustments and careful listening, followed by more rounds of feedback, until the note was just right.

Not many people had the stomach for this high-level degree of problem-solving. But it was different for the young man — he felt a deep sense of ownership that drove him to make his product work. His behaviour demonstrated a level of grit that he did not know he had — it was certainly not something he had experienced while working in real estate. It was through the school tasting sessions that Vita Milk started gaining a reputation for nutrition while evolving its taste with each school it was trialled at.

The school experiment was successful. With government support, Vita Milk began to be distributed to schools and expanded its service area a year later. The improvement in sales and guaranteed orders from schools meant sales had increased from 300–400 bottles per day to around 1000 by 1941. It was a significant win, not only because of the increase in sales, but also because it allowed the young man to continue tinkering with the taste. As the service area expanded, the young man saw an opportunity to implement the same model that had worked so well in the refugee camp, but on a larger scale — he set up a distribution centre, which would serve both as a warehouse and a Vita Milk café. The dual-purpose facility was a clever move as it combined a platform for direct customer feedback with only limited additional cost; Vita Milk was readily available at the distribution centre. The cost of running the café was minimal and its benefit was immense. It was a demonstration of smart strategic allocation.

It soon became obvious that Vita Milk appealed to younger drinkers who had trialled the taste, or who had seen it at their schools and told their friends about it. They gathered at the café, which looked more like an afterthought that had been attached to the main distribution centre. Its popularity contradicted its unappealing exterior and reconfirmed that the strategy of targeting students was the path with the highest probability of success.

One year into the launch of his company, there were many positive signs. For starters, he had established some traction with his target demographic and had growing support from government to continue the school program. Although some remnants of the beany flavour remained, the taste was substantially improved from the early days owing to the feedback gathered from school tastings and the distribution centre café. Despite the revenue generated from selling 1000 bottles per day helping to slow the cash burn, the business continued to deplete funds and remained well below the break-even point. The trend in demand indicated that at some point in the future the business would eventually be able to support itself, but there was no indication of when exactly this would be. By this time, the young founder had invested HK$30000 (equivalent to approximately US$70000 as at 2020) of his own personal funds. He knew he needed to invest more to see the initial period through.

And what about the second issue of fixing Vita Milk's short shelf life? Despite the good intentions and effort of all involved, the issue would persist without any solution for many more years. In fact, the company would go broke at the start of the Second World War as it could not support the drop in sales following the Japanese invasion. In an ironic twist, the young man would be forced to flee to China as a refugee during the Japanese invasion.

He and his young family survived the Japanese occupation of Hong Kong by drinking soybean milk in a Chinese refugee camp. It would strengthen his bond with soybean milk. In the back of his mind, he desperately wanted another chance at resurrecting the business. Just as an unfinished novel begs to be picked up again, the issue of improving the shelf life remained as a 'to be continued' in his subconscious.

The surrender of Japan in 1944 was a sign that fate wanted him to continue his work — or at least he took it that way. With gusto, he returned to his factory and was pleasantly surprised to find it undamaged and in a good state. What possessed him to dedicate the energy to rebuild the business is something only a founder can understand. He borrowed HK$50 000 from a friend, and Vita Milk was up and running again.

There was very little competition during this time. Hong Kong was reestablishing itself and by seizing the opportunity, he was able to grow sales exponentially. His only competitors were soft drink companies, which were a totally different offering because of differences in taste and nutritional value. Sales were booming and he now had the capital and time to strategically allocate to solve the bigger issue at hand — how to increase the shelf life of Vita Milk. By hiring an expert in dairy science, he approached the problem like he always did. And just like tuning a guitar, his team finally figured out how to use soft drink bottles to store the product without refrigeration. It was a breakthrough well worth the 12-year wait. It was 1953 when Vita Milk really took off. Sales continued to double, then double again as if the long-life solution unlocked a whole new surge in demand.

By now, you may have surmised that this origin story is that of Vitasoy International Holdings, today a company listed in Hong Kong but having expanded into China, Singapore, and the Philippines. Dr Kwee-Seong Lo, who founded the business, was a pioneer of Hong Kong business and trade during the Japanese occupation of Hong Kong. He developed a strong interest in historical Chinese ceramics, and later in life became a keen supporter of biomedical research and philanthropy. The Lo family still retain significant ownership in the business today and remain on the board.

It is only through this deep sense of ownership that Dr Kwee-Seong Lo rebuilt his business following the war. He sacrificed his career and took on personal loans during uncertain times because he believed in the business. His actions reflected both a desire to succeed and a carefully considered strategic allocation that focused on improving the shelf life of the product so he could unlock its full potential. And most interestingly, this is a clear example of the power of psychological ownership.

Dr Kwee-Seong Lo's journey is a story about motivation — the invisible drive that pushes people to persevere even in the face of extreme adversity. There are many times in this story where our hero could have given up. But he did not. Why? What motivated him to push on? What does his story tell us about motivators and incentives? As Charlie Munger once said, 'Show me the incentives, and I'll show you the outcome.' The incentives that drive us to strive for a long-term reward are distinctly different and, oftentimes, opposed to what is comfortable in the short term. Many executives contracted to five-to-seven-year terms have no incentive to employ strategies aimed at the next decade. But the Vitasoy example shows us how Dr Kwee-Seong Lo achieved outcomes that are only possible with a long-term mindset and a sense of psychological ownership that comes from intrinsic motivation.

Equally, it is not ideal to rely solely on intrinsic motivation as the way to build alignment with executives. In today's environment, few executives would be content with only the internal satisfaction derived from their work. A balanced approach is necessary, combining sufficient extrinsic motivation with strong intrinsic motivation. The key here is 'sufficient'. An excessive focus on external motivators, such as high remuneration, can actually diminish intrinsic motivation. Research has shown that excessive financial incentives can in fact contaminate the psychological impact of intrinsic motivation.[6-8] This is a story we have seen come true throughout corporate history — a CEO that starts their tenure with modest remuneration achieves success by thinking like an owner, only to fade in the latter half of their tenure as they become the victim of their growing remuneration package. Focus turns to securing personal key performance indicators (KPIs), and the company is left no better off than when it first started.

The result of Dr Kwee-Seong Lo's motivation to succeed is a multi-decade journey that created immense wealth for him, his future generations, and those that had the foresight to back him. In the following chapters, I take you through the concept of alignment in more detail, and explore how outsiders can identify the makings of an effective executive incentive scheme.

CHAPTER 4

Extrinsic motivators: Effective incentives

In this chapter, we explore the elements of an effective remuneration scheme. How can extrinsic motivators be used by owners and directors to align executive management with company goals? These external drivers push executives to succeed, are visible to outsiders, and are largely in the control of directors and owners. A well-crafted incentive plan can mark the difference between a CEO who adopts a risk-averse approach, focusing on defending their current market to meet short-term targets, and a CEO who opts for bold investments that could unlock new growth potential, even if they impact short-term profits. Both CEOs may have similar experience and talent, but their decisions will be shaped by their underlying motivations.

The very purpose of corporate incentives is to strengthen the bond between directors, executives, and shareholders, and to motivate executives and directors to behave as though they are the owners of the business. Shareholders care about long-term performance and growth. Their payoff is in the form of stock price appreciation and receipt of dividends, both of which only come to fruition when a company is growing and profitable. Shareholders stand to lose the most as they are not paid a salary like directors and executives—ultimately, their personal capital is at risk if the company does not continue to perform. In contrast, directors and executives receive a guaranteed salary irrespective of company performance. Therein lies the asymmetric payoff that short-term incentives (such as bonuses) and long-term incentives (such as stock options) seek to address. These incentives are intended to enhance the bond with shareholders so that directors and executives can feel the upside or downside of company performance alongside the company's shareholders. The intention is to motivate actions and behaviours for the long term. However, this conventional approach overlooks key psychological aspects of human motivation because of its myopic focus on remuneration in isolation.

While remuneration is the primary and most significant extrinsic factor, there are other elements that investors, executives, and directors should consider. A more modern and comprehensive approach to extrinsic motivation, which incorporates the science of psychology, involves looking at the full range of factors that can influence the mindset of executive managers. In this chapter, I explore how companies make effective use of extrinsic motivators to align with both the company's and owners' goals, and how outsiders can spot a well-designed incentive structure.

Different types of extrinsic motivators

Companies have more ways to reward employees than pure financial incentives. Some of these factors may align with the company's interests, while others may cater more to personal benefits for executives. Together, they provide a broader understanding of what drives an executive team.

Financial incentives

Financial incentive schemes have been studied extensively.[1] They play a fundamental role in any motivation strategy, serving as a key component of the overall framework.

The balance between base salary, bonuses, and stock options is a perennial topic of great interest at shareholder meetings. This type of motivation is one most readers will associate with remuneration schemes adopted by boards and shareholders. The primary goal of these remuneration structures is to create alignment between short-term and long-term interests, ensuring that executive managers are motivated to drive sustainable growth for shareholders over the long term. In the extreme, some executives choose to skew their incentives heavily towards the long term, opting to pay themselves a de minimis base salary and instead rely on generating personal financial benefit purely from their ownership stake in the company. Famous examples include Warren Buffett of Berkshire Hathaway, who receives US$100000 a year in base salary, and Michael Cannon-Brookes of Atlassian Corp, who receives US$50000 per annum. A low base salary is uncommon but more typical in founder-led companies due to the founders' substantial equity ownership. By choosing this approach, founders send a strong signal to the market while also aligning their interests with shareholders, as their main financial rewards come from their equity stake in the company.

Career advancement

It is human nature to seek growth and new challenges, and executives are no exception. Their ambitious personalities, shaped by a focus on achievement, naturally view success as a form of reward. For C-suite managers, the progression they seek is usually in the form of attaining a larger portfolio within their remit, leading a larger organisation, or becoming a director and building a board portfolio.

This desire is natural and often drives executives to work hard to meet the key performance indicators (KPIs) set for them. This motivation is aligned with owners and directors when management teams are cohesive, with a clear understanding of each member's role and their contribution to the overall success of the team. However, this motivator breaks down when executive teams become dysfunctional. Many companies have been derailed by executives vying for career advancement in teams where roles are unclear, free-riding occurs, and internal conflicts arise. This can lead to territorial disputes, with executives focusing on self-serving, 'career-defining' projects that enhance their résumés rather than benefiting the company in the long run. Think of executives that guard their divisions tightly, seeing other executives as rivals. Others may lobby for nonsensical projects that serve only to enhance their personal glory while draining company resources.

Ego

Ego and prestige should never be underestimated when it comes to corporate motivation. In small doses this can lead to ambition and growth, but many prominent business figures have met their downfall as a result of letting their ego surpass logic and common sense. Executives that are excessively driven by ego do not make great long-term management decisions as common sense can be overshadowed by the desire to further their individual prominence and recognition. Nevertheless, recognition, fame, and similar aspirations are a legitimate driving force for some. The question is: What do these business figures want to be recognised for?

If the desire to be in the limelight is aligned with the long-term interests of the company, then this can be of great benefit. Bill Ackman, the activist hedge fund manager and founder of Pershing Square, has used his media presence to advocate for corporate change by putting pressure on companies in Pershing Square's portfolio. This desire for recognition was closely aligned with his activist style of investing when he aggressively advocated for corporate change in target companies. Contrast this with Bob Iger, CEO of Disney, who has built his media profile from a string of bold acquisitions, including the US$71 billion acquisition of 21st Century Fox—some have questioned his motives and whether this acquisition was beneficial for Disney shareholders or more a vehicle for Iger to cement his corporate legacy.

The question outsiders should ask is: Does ego motivate the executive team to elevate the company's brand alongside their own, or does the evidence point to a more individualistic focus?

Competition

Executive managers are high achievers accustomed to high levels of competition. In certain industries, however, rivalries emerge that transcend the usual level of competition. These companies repeatedly encounter each other in multiple product lines, driving a heightened level of desire within their respective management teams to outdo their counterparts. Steve Jobs, co-founder of Apple, was renowned for his desire to beat Bill Gates and Microsoft. Marc Benioff, a former executive of Oracle, left the company to start Salesforce with the blessing of Oracle's founder and CEO Larry Ellison. Ellison even mentored Benioff while he was at Oracle, and in the early days of Salesforce, Ellison provided initial capital and was a board director. The relationship deteriorated after it was revealed that Oracle was working to develop a competitor product, kick-starting a well-publicised rivalry that has continued for decades.

The motivational benefits of competition were first observed by Norman Triplett in 1898, who found that cyclists produced faster times under direct competition as opposed to racing alone or with a pacesetter. It is not surprising that performance improves with the presence of competition, but in a study published in 2014,[2] Gavin Kilduff went further to establish that rivals (competitors with a regular history of going head-to-head and who know each other) perform even better when compared to competitors who had no prior relationship. We see this motivational effect play out in hyper-competitive industries such as cloud computing, consumer electronics, and social media platforms. As generative artificial intelligence (AI) becomes more widespread, we can expect rivalries and competition to spur the performance of executive managers in this industry.

The fundamentals of executive remuneration

Remuneration reports often appear overly complex, filled with pages of text and intricate details. However, this complexity reflects the significance of financial incentives and their critical role in aligning executives' interests with those of the company's owners. Alongside base salaries, it is common to see performance bonuses, stock options, restricted stock units, and long-term incentive plans, with each tranche having individual triggers and vesting periods. For outsiders, the key to understanding these reports is to focus on the fundamentals, guided by principles of motivational psychology, rather than getting bogged down in the intricate details. The primary questions to ask are: Is the total compensation in a reasonable market range, and do the executive incentives genuinely foster long-term alignment with the company's goals?

Balancing short- and long-term incentives

Not all financial incentives are equal, and some are more compelling motivators than others. The ideal structure for long-term wealth creation is fostered when executive managers are driven by the right motivations. As outsiders, we are interested in gauging how aligned management executives are to their shareholders. Almost always, there should be a skew towards long-term incentives. Base salaries and annual bonuses are short term in nature and therefore should be kept within reasonable bounds. Most companies typically conduct a benchmarking exercise to ascertain the 50th percentile base salary, comparing it to their closest competitors. This level would be considered 'at market'. Whether the board decides to compensate above the market level is a separate decision. In most cases, overly generous salaries and annual bonuses are less effective as long-term motivators and can undermine intrinsic drivers. While such incentives can be valuable for attracting talent in a competitive market, once executives are on board, excessive short-term rewards often lead to short-sighted decision-making. In most jurisdictions, what is considered 'at market' is more than enough.

If in a competitive hiring situation executive managers demand an excessively high base salary, it puts into question their underlying motivators. Instead, long-term financial incentives such as stock options and restricted stock units should constitute the larger proportion of executive remuneration. Prolonging the time before executive compensation is paid allows more time for growth strategies to come to fruition. The judgement of the success or failure of management skills and strategies is rarely demonstrated over an annual timeframe.

For example, if we examine the remuneration structure of Marriott from its 2024 Proxy Statement, we can see there are five key executives with base salaries ranging from US$700000 through to US$1.4 million.[3] These ranges are not excessive and have been benchmarked at the 50th percentile level independently according to the proxy statement. A sense check of competitor proxy statements can also quickly confirm their reasonableness. Next, we look for the balance between short-term and long-term incentives—a review of the summary table within the proxy statement shows us that for all executives, the value of deferred incentives materially exceeds the value of immediately realisable incentives.[3] A check of the stock-based awards is necessary to determine the timing of when these vest, and the majority of the value is realised in a three-year window. As an outsider, we would prefer a longer horizon, but if we balance this with the significant skew towards deferred stock-based compensation, it presents as a favourable mix. Combined with the fact that base salaries are within a reasonable range, all in all, and while not perfect, Marriott's incentive structure is sufficiently aligned with the long-term interests of shareholders.

As a related point, outsiders may find reassurance in knowing that David Marriott serves as Chair, holds a 10 per cent ownership stake, and is the founder's grandson—someone we anticipate will have oversight over executive compensation.

Stretching the time horizon

The purpose of any deferred (or vested) incentives such as restricted stock awards is to encourage executives to deliver strategies that have a prolonged benefit for the company. Typically, deferral periods range from three to five years. Most of the large multinational corporations adopt these timeframes to stay competitive in the hiring market and attract talented executives (the executives themselves would obviously prefer to have a shorter deferral period). But the deferral period itself should be used as a method to discover those managers that have a willingness to back themselves over the long term, versus those that are only confident in their abilities over a short period of time. The ideal design is to extend the deferral period to at least seven years (the average tenure of a CEO), combined with an outsized reward at the end of the period. This design replicates the compounding nature of returns if one owned the company—if the strategy of executive management is sound and executed well, the value of the company grows in an exponential fashion as opposed to a linear fashion. This return profile, akin to a hockey stick, should be what motivates executives, not the linear return (which is the result of shorter time horizons).

For the power of compounding to truly take effect, a sufficiently long timeframe is necessary for meaningful results. Paycom, a US-based human resources software company, exemplified this when it set an eight-year vesting window for its newly appointed Co-CEO in 2024. This structure encourages a focus on long-term growth strategies that extend well beyond the typical three-to-five-year horizon. Additionally, Paycom's founder and other Co-CEO has been given a 10-year vesting window, tied to an extraordinary potential payout exceeding US$300 million if ambitious share price targets are met.[4]

While these lengthy, high-stakes incentives are controversial, they can drive bold, transformative decisions when implemented effectively. Paycom's management team is already showing signs of this with the launch of a self-managed payroll product, which, despite short-term profit cannibalisation, could revolutionise payroll processing and fuel the company's next phase of growth. Additionally, their global expansion strategy aims to significantly boost market share. Should these goals be realised, both executives and shareholders stand to benefit from substantial share price appreciation.

Executive KPIs: Look beyond the financial targets

Most executive remuneration plans focus on financial results because they are objective and easy to measure. They also happen to be very short term in nature. But what is often overlooked is the importance of delivering growth in areas that will outlast the executive team. For example, the enhancement of the brand, reputation, and philosophy of the company should be of great interest to owners, and therefore executive managers should be incentivised in the same way to create alignment. These elements build on the foundation of a company, whereas financial results vary from year to year. Sure, most companies have a mission statement—but are these ideals truly adhered to? Does the management team truly believe in the company's vision? The executives that do so and can demonstrate it to employees and customers will have true influence (more on that in Part 3). These are the companies that reap the long-term benefits of a recognisable and trustworthy brand—which, unlike financial results, can propel the business along a much larger runway.

While the issue of brand building may seem like an abstract, subjective topic, let me illustrate this by sharing the story of a company that has differentiated itself and built its success on a simple philosophy—what it calls *humanistic capital*. This is more than just an esoteric mission statement as it genuinely permeates throughout the operations of the company. For decades, this company has incentivised its executive management team to build upon its brand and assessed the performance of the team on more than just financial results. In doing so, this company has demonstrated phenomenal growth in the very competitive luxury clothing industry. Importantly, shareholders have benefited immensely along the way.

Aligned for the future: Brunello Cucinelli

Brunello Cucinelli is a luxury clothing brand originating from northern Italy. It was founded by its namesake Mr Brunello Cucinelli in 1978. Over the course of almost 50 years, Mr Cucinelli has created a company culture that has elevated its brand to become synonymous with craftsmanship, sustainability, and ethical capitalism.

Economically it has been a phenomenon. Since listing in 2012, it has grown its market capitalisation from €527 million to over €7 billion in 2024. This has been achieved by prioritising brand building activities ahead of short-term profits. When other luxury clothing brands were focused on competing for quality and allure, Brunello Cucinelli was developing another angle. It engaged in strategic initiatives that enhanced its reputation for sustainability and ethical manufacturing. This emphasis is reflected in its executive remuneration KPIs. A close examination of its executive management performance targets[5] shows its philosophy of humanistic capitalism is more than just rhetoric:

- Economic: 50 per cent linked to group turnover

- Environmental, Social, Governance (ESG): 50 per cent linked to its Sustainability Plan, development of its Carbon Disclosure Project, implementation of its Sustainable Supply Chain project, developing the environmental impact calculation for its supply chain.

Brunello Cucinelli has not been a trend follower that has jumped on the ESG train in recent times. ESG has been core to its brand proposition for decades and is the reason it has differentiated itself from other luxury brands — the philosophy behind its ESG approach is motivated by value creation and brand building. Structuring the performance metrics in this way aligns executive management with wealth creation in the long-term interests of its owners. This is core to the Brunello Cucinelli brand proposition.

What does humanistic capitalism mean to Brunello Cucinelli and its shareholders? How does a profit-seeking listed company promote humanistic capitalism in a genuine way that generates wealth? Are these concepts mutually exclusive? The company has written extensively on its ethical philosophy, which is underpinned by a fundamental belief that it is possible to generate a fair profit while giving back to the community and prioritising respect for people and their economic dignity.[6] Judging by the growth of the company, this concept works. It is not just a mere construct of a philosophical nirvana. It marries cohesively with the brand's interpretation of a quiet luxury lifestyle — a stark difference to the often loud and overtly hedonistic marketing of most luxury brands. In the early 2000s, the company strategically purchased a large plot of land that housed an old industrial factory in the Solomeo Valley near Tuscany. The factory was run down, but its surroundings were pristine and an ideal location for nearby Italian artisans. After significant capital expenditure to revitalise the factory, a campus-style headquarters was built that maintained the beauty and character of the old historic buildings. This was a strategic project to establish a best-in-class factory aimed at attracting and retaining artisan talent and leveraging the 'Made in Italy' tag synonymous with quality and craftsmanship — humanistic capitalism at work. Had performance metrics focused on financial results alone, the painstakingly careful restoration of each building would not have been undertaken. The pursuit of a light-filled, bright, modern factory would not have made any short-term financial sense. But half of executive management performance is judged on brand-building activities. And from this perspective, the factory campus in the Solomeo Valley, which has been dubbed the Hamlet of Cashmere and Harmony by Brunello Cucinelli, has proven to be the centrepiece of its brand, representing the value it places on beautiful workplaces that elevate the dignity of its employees. The company's headquarters at Solomeo Valley have featured heavily in its marketing material and no doubt been a key contributor to the company's reputation. From a long-term perspective, it is an investment that makes perfect sense.

Another example is the continual investment Brunello Cucinelli has made in sustainability. It provides a garment repair service, which in 2023 repaired 3 400 items of clothing. It would be much easier not to offer the service. The costs of administration, transportation, and logistics would ordinarily yield minimal financial benefit to the company. But that is not the way the performance metrics have been set. The recent implementation of improved logistics and transportation software has been an investment designed to improve inventory management and hence reduce carbon emissions, as has the use of recycled cardboard for its entire packaging of hung clothing. And most recently, it has launched a supply chain digital ID mapping initiative designed to trace through the entire production chain so that the environmental impact can be broken down into granular detail.

Brunello Cucinelli has cleverly tied its brand to quiet luxury and a concept it terms 'humanistic capitalism'. But importantly, non-financial performance metrics have been set in a way that requires the executive management team to build on that brand persona. It has sacrificed short-term financial results to pursue these initiatives, but gradually over the course of decades these actions have accumulated into a brand that is now differentiated and compelling for customers, and desirable to employees.

CHAPTER 5

Intrinsic motivators: The intangible driver

Children can be incentivised to complete their homework with treats and presents, but those that truly excel at school are usually self-driven. Likewise for executives, extrinsic motivators, such as financial incentives, career advancement, ego, and competition, will only take a company so far. The typical corporate business model assumes that motivation is primarily driven by financial reward, when in fact that is only a fraction of what motivates individuals and teams.

In psychological terms, financial incentives are classified as extrinsic factors because they are external rewards—benefits and rewards offered to executives once a key performance indicator (KPI) is achieved; that is, the traditional carrot and stick approach—and the key driver is external to the executive or manager. The missing element of motivation in these cases is the understanding and harnessing of *intrinsic motivation*.[1] This is defined as motivation that originates from within, often in relation to one's own curiosity and yearning to achieve, improve, and learn. Combine that extrinsic financial reward with something more, something *intrinsic*, and that is when an unstoppable enduring drive arises. That same drive that is almost always found in founders.

One of the pioneers of motivational psychology, Edward L Deci, conducted the famous Soma Cube experiment to measure the impact of intrinsic motivation versus extrinsic motivation.[2] He divided college students into two groups and placed them in separate rooms. Each room had a pile of magazines to the side, and each student was given a Soma Cube puzzle to solve (see figure 5-1). This puzzle involves seven polycubes, all of different shapes, that can together be assembled into a 3 x 3 x 3 cube using the correct configuration of the cubes. There are 240 different solutions to the puzzle. He instructed one group that they would be paid for each solution they completed, while the other group of students were simply asked to complete the puzzle with no mention of payment or reward.

Figure 5-1: The Soma Cube puzzle.

After a certain period of time, Deci announced that the puzzle-solving time was over and that he needed to leave for about 10 minutes to gather data, promising to return with a questionnaire. He left the room, then observed the behaviour of the two groups. Those students who were paid to complete the puzzle (extrinsically motivated) all largely stopped, and began looking at the magazines, whereas those that were not promised a reward (and therefore intrinsically motivated) continued working on the puzzles of their own volition while waiting for Deci's return. This experiment, along with countless studies that followed over the years, effectively illustrates the effects of intrinsic motivation.

At a neuroscientific level, further studies[3] have shown a strong linkage between the positive experiences associated with exploration and new learning, and higher levels of dopamine. In other words, dopamine, the reward hormone of our brain, is activated when our intrinsic motivators are activated.

In this chapter, I show how executive teams driven by intrinsic motivators will exhibit a different type of drive when it comes to solving business challenges. Expect greater persistence, interest, and creativity—put simply, intrinsic motivators are a prerequisite for effectively motivated and aligned executive teams.

The science of intrinsic motivation

So, what are these magical intrinsic motivators we speak of, that can unlock long-term value not only in management teams, but also individuals? Purpose. Mastery. Autonomy.[4] These values-based, internal psychological drivers form the foundation of deep-rooted intrinsic motivation. They are what fuel us to push beyond the ordinary, seeking not external rewards but the personal satisfaction that comes from growth and fulfilment.

Interestingly, I experienced the power of these motivators firsthand during the COVID-19 pandemic. Like many in the lead up to the pandemic, I found myself in a busy routine—work, family, life—caught up in the day-to-day without a conscious thought on purpose and curiosity. But lockdown had an unexpected twist: it gave me autonomy. With my regular schedule disrupted and certain obligations paused, I found myself with the mental space and freedom I hadn't realised I needed.

One rainy afternoon, I stumbled upon an old guitar I'd bought my wife years ago while we were dating, intending to serenade her. The guitar had long since gathered dust, a symbol of a plan never realised. But in that newfound headspace, I picked it up again, thinking perhaps I could lift my wife's spirits during quarantine. That sense of purpose reignited a spark in me. Over the following months, I dedicated myself to mastering her favourite instrumental, diving into instructional videos and practising whenever I could.

Through this experience, I rediscovered how powerful intrinsic motivators can be. The autonomy to choose how to spend my time gave way to a renewed sense of purpose. And with that purpose, came the drive to achieve mastery. Just don't ask me to play another song.

Purpose

Perhaps the most powerful of intrinsic motivators, Richard M Ryan and Edward L Deci's research on self-determination theory looks at intrinsic motivation being tied to the basic psychological need for 'relatedness'. This concept originates from the inherent human desire to find a sense of purpose in the activities they engage in. That is, an individual feels more connected to an activity when they perceive a deeper meaning to the activity that aligns with their internal values and belief systems. The sense of relatedness arises through this connection between the task and their personal values—as a result, they are more committed to and engaged with the task.

Studies have gone on to show that meaningful and purposeful work can significantly enhance employee motivation and engagement. This is even more important at the executive level if a company hopes to achieve alignment through the intrinsic and extrinsic motivators it offers.

Mastery

Another key component of intrinsic motivation and self-determination theory is the concept of competence and mastery—that is, the internal drive an individual has to learn and improve, ultimately achieving mastery in their capabilities. This stems from their desire for personal growth and is fuelled by feelings of satisfaction when achieving a skill or competency.

In one research study,[5] participants given challenging tasks that emphasised personal growth and skill development demonstrated higher levels of motivation and persistence when compared to those given tasks that were more outcome-oriented. This study showed when individuals perceive tasks as opportunities to develop and enhance their abilities (rather than just to perform well), their intrinsic motivation is significantly increased.

The pursuit of mastery—driven by the desire to refine a skill or achieve proficiency—fuels sustained engagement and effort, exemplifying the power of mastery as an intrinsic motivator. In a business context, particularly with executive teams, this motivator may seem less apparent and is often overlooked. Senior leaders are typically assumed to already possess the necessary skills for their roles, making skill acquisition less of a focus. However, by assigning executives challenging responsibilities and holding them objectively accountable for their outcomes, we can actively harness this powerful intrinsic motivator to drive performance. One example is reassigning executives to a different portfolio, requiring them to crossover into new areas and embrace fresh opportunities for mastery. This not only reignites their sense of accomplishment but also helps counter the cognitive biases discussed in Chapter 3.

Autonomy

When individuals have the freedom to choose and control their actions, they are more likely to be intrinsically motivated. Self-determination theory tells us autonomy is fundamental to intrinsic motivation, and a key enabler for engaging in activities that are meaningful and fulfilling (and therefore tied to purpose and mastery). Autonomy and the self-direction of engaging in a task facilitates a person to pursue activities that align with their personal values, hence intrinsic motivation is significantly influenced by the experience of autonomy.

A well-known real-world example of this is software company Atlassian's 'ShipIt Days'. Every quarter, Atlassian employees and executives have the freedom to work on anything of their choice for 24 hours, presenting their work back to their respective teams. This taps into an individual's desire for autonomy while linking that motivator to the organisation's benefit.

Imagine you are the owner

Rather than providing a theoretical explanation of what it means for management to behave like owners, allow me to illustrate the hidden superpower of psychological ownership by way of examples from the various founder-led companies I have encountered over the years. These companies, through the leadership of their founders, demonstrate the application of both intrinsic and extrinsic motivators in effective moderation, achieving powerful alignment.

Ikigai: A reason for being

Imagine you are wandering through a bustling Japanese market on a crisp autumn morning. The air is filled with the fragrant aroma of freshly brewed tea and the distant, soothing strains of a shamisen. You are drawn to a quaint stall where an elderly man is gently but skilfully kneading dough. Lines softly decorate the corners of his eyes as he offers a welcoming smile. The scent of freshly baked bread wafts through the air. The man is renowned for his shokupan and crowds of all ages eagerly line up for a warm loaf to take home. His loaves often sell out before midday, and each day, as he closes up shop, he does so with a deep sense of fulfilment, knowing he is contributing to his community. His loaves are more than just food; they offer comfort and joy to those who enjoy them.

He has found his reason for being – his *ikigai*. His reason for waking up each day with a sense of purpose and delight. His skills align with his love, enabling him to fulfil a need for his community.

I once visited a founder-led company called AIT at its Osaka head office. It operated in logistics—typically considered a boring, slow-growing industry. But what caught my attention with AIT was its ability to produce consistent earnings growth over very long periods of time. In fact, it had been able to increase its earnings and dividends tenfold from 2008 to 2024.

As the lift opened and I walked into its company headquarters in downtown Osaka, I was surprised to find a cramped and small office with a particularly unimpressive reception area. It was reminiscent of those old 1980s offices where you could picture a cigarette-smoking boss in front of cream-coloured walls. I thought I had entered the wrong office. Just before I was about to turn around, I was promptly greeted and asked to sit in a reception area that felt more like a doctor's office than a company that was turning over close to US$400 million a year. I did not mind it, though. The company was obviously not spending its capital on swish offices — another hallmark of a founder-led company.

From my initial research, I knew the company's founder still owned about a third of the company. As a CEO in his 70s, he was old for Western standards, but he had remained as CEO since founding the company in 1995. The question for me was not about his age (we have seen leaders of the free world much older than that), but rather his energy and alignment with shareholders.

I was eventually greeted by a senior manager who turned out to have been with the company for 15 years and was employee number 20. He was the perfect host — he had the long history with the company, direct and to the point, unrehearsed in all his answers and delivered with quintessential Japanese patience. He answered all the questions I had for him. Did the founder have energy? That was a resounding yes. Yagura-san was a sprightly 76-year-old with the personality of a young kid (this was how they described him). He had no wife and kids, and he dedicated most of his waking hours to the business. I was told he only took one week of leave each year — an annual fishing trip to Wakayama was enough to recharge the batteries. His original goal had been to take the company to listing. Now that it had been achieved, his next goal was to continue with AIT's international expansion. He was thinking about the next horizon of growth, which would come from acquiring small logistics companies in specific target countries. It was his life's passion to continue growing the business.

He also believed in uncompromised financial stability, which is why the company carried little debt—a trait common with founder-led companies, as they believe in being in control of one's own destiny and not being subject to financial covenants from lenders. His second-in-charge, the managing director, had been with the company for over 25 years and he too owned about 4 per cent of the company, accumulated over the course of the decades of his involvement. He exuded the very concept of *ikigai* through his leadership of AIT—passion, use of his talents in growing a business, building something the world needs, and clearly generating a financial return for it.

The long game requires sacrifice

In theory, it sounds easy to be a founder, manager, and owner. In reality, a great deal of sacrifices may need to be made. Only those with a genuine sense of ownership are willing to make those sacrifices. When I met with the team at HyVision System in Korea, I learned that CEO and founder Doowon Choi lived near the office, while his wife and family lived in downtown Seoul, located 1.5 hours away. Being close to the office meant he would only see his family on Sundays, when he would attend church and spend the rest of the day with them.

He founded the company at the age of 32, and today the business counts Samsung and Apple as customers (developing testing equipment for cameras and sensors critical to smartphone applications, such as augmented reality). He had grown the company from scratch into a US$200 million market cap global business over the course of two decades while retaining 14 per cent ownership. An impressive feat, but one which required significant personal sacrifice that would not be visible on the surface. That demonstrates the work ethic and dedication required to compete on a global scale.

As a side anecdote to this story, when I asked about his succession plans, I was informed his children would be unlikely candidates to succeed their father. They were planning on becoming K-pop stars.

Nothing is below a founder

In contexts where the balance between extrinsic and intrinsic motivators is skewed too much toward extrinsic motivators, executive management teams can often become too focused on ego to partake in activities that are beneficial to the business. Take the small example of business-to-business engagement; in large organisations with multiple hierarchies, senior leaders will often only engage with their equivalently senior counterpart at another business. They will not afford their time to junior staffers. This may be driven by practical reasons; however, this can have a negative impact on business.

Chemist Warehouse is Australia's largest pharmacy chain, which grew from one store in 1972 in the outer suburbs of Melbourne into a group with over 500 stores generating annual revenues of US$2 billion today. In a conversation with Jack Gance,[6,7] one of the co-founders and majority shareholders, it became apparent to me what was so starkly unique about his ownership mindset. Psychological ownership for Jack means staying close to his customers and paying attention to detail.

Jack relayed the story about one of his key suppliers, a global vitamin and supplements manufacturer that supplies his stores. Typically, the buying team at Chemist Warehouse liaises with the sales team from the vitamin manufacturer to decide the quantity and types of products it will buy. The 'buyers' in Chemist Warehouse, although not in senior management, are valued members of Jack's team who are highly experienced and well paid. They are key influencers whose decisions also determine how much revenue the vitamin manufacturer will make from Chemist Warehouse. From what I understood of the conversation, it sounded like Chemist Warehouse represents a significant portion of revenues for the vitamin manufacturer, and therefore Jack's buyers were very important to the manufacturer. To emphasise the importance of Chemist Warehouse to the vitamin manufacturer, he told me a story.

One day, in conversation with the vitamin CEO, Jack asked the CEO if he knew the buyer at Chemist Warehouse.

The vitamin CEO replied that he did not.

Jack asked if the CEO knew the buyer from a major supermarket chain (another one of the vitamin manufacturer's customers).

He didn't. Feeling the pointedness of Jack's line of questioning, the CEO explained that he knew the counterpart CEOs, but he felt he should not be expected to know the individual buyers of his customers. He had sales teams for that.

Jack found this mindset completely foreign — he couldn't understand how a CEO wouldn't personally know the key decision-makers of such a critical customer, especially since Chemist Warehouse and the supermarket accounted for a significant portion of the vitamin company's revenue. If it were Jack, he said, he would absolutely cultivate close relationships with the key buyers who drive those decisions. As he puts it, 'business is a person-to-person interface, not numbers-to-numbers'.

When I met Jack he was in his 70s, but his demeanour was more akin to a man in his 50s. Psychological ownership is an invisible driver that compels him to stay close to his customers. If he needs to roll up his sleeves, he does it without question. He still studies weekly sales reports for each store and strategises about the products he needs to stock and which suburbs he needs to expand into. A founder is not blinded by ego; they see the importance of engaging with staffers at all levels. No task (nor person) is below a founder.

The wisdom of conservative cash management

Many managers with a sense of psychological ownership view their personal wealth as being directly correlated with the company. Metaphorically, much like a married couple that shares a bank account, these executives manage business cash prudently, often minimising the amount of debt and other borrowings. They prefer to keep cash for reinvestment in the business, and carefully consider expenditures that waste company capital. They behave as though the success of the company is intertwined with the trajectory of their personal wealth. They do not seek to extract wealth from the company by paying themselves an exorbitant salary because, to them, there is no delineation between personal and business.

On a visit to Spigen's headquarters in Seoul, I learned about its culture of frugality and conservative cash management. For context, Spigen is a US$150 million market cap global company that sells innovative mobile phone accessories, yet its executives fly economy class. Staff strategy offsite meetings involve overseas travel, but the CEO & Founder, consistent with all employees, share hotel rooms to keep costs down. While Spigen's approach is quite extreme, there are other companies with a similar conservative philosophy that take a slightly different route: they choose never to incur any debt. Barry Lambert, CEO and founder of Count Financial, told me he once took out a working capital facility and only discovered the interest rate was 20.5 per cent per annum after he called the bank (this was in the 1980s, when it was not a requirement for Australian banks to disclose the interest rate).

He paid it off immediately and decided he would never take out another business loan ever again.[8] The same goes for Jack Gance (co-founder of Chemist Warehouse) and Graham Turner (CEO and founder of Flight Centre Group), who both avoid using debt finance.

An executive career built with psychological ownership

Back in 2008, a 47-year-old Vice President quit Cisco to join a start-up no one had heard of. She had spent the previous 15 years at Cisco, which at the time was a giant of the industry. The move raised a few eyebrows because Cisco was turning over billions of dollars each year, but this unknown start-up had only been running for four years and had virtually no revenue.[9] It had the tongue-twisting name of Arastra. What would possess someone at the height of their career to quit and join an unknown? To risk a high-paying, comfortable job for a start-up that was measuring revenue in US$10 000 intervals?

For starters, she was joining as the CEO and a member of the board — the career advancement motivated her. Not only that, but the move also excited her because compared to Cisco, her career trajectory was not already predetermined. Here was a blank sheet of paper where she could carve out a new legacy and be there to influence the outcome from the ground floor up. There was a sense of autonomy. She knew the computer networking industry well and believed she could apply that expertise to a new challenger in the industry. On the other hand, at a multi-billion-dollar company like Cisco, career progression was already set — she had joined Cisco in its early days and saw the immense growth of the technology industry through the boom in the 1990s, followed by the crash in the early 2000s, and then the slow rebuild in the early 2000s. Cisco had grown from a small company, and now the bureaucracy was beginning to creep in — it had grown into something that did not fit with her long-term goals. The culture had changed and when she reflected deeply, she no longer saw herself retiring there — she realised she was going through the motions. So, when a former colleague at Cisco informed her they were seeking a CEO for their four-year-old start-up, she jumped at the opportunity to link back up with someone she respected and had known for 20 years.

Within the first month as CEO, she thought she had hit a home run by securing a big investment bank as a flagship customer. It was Lehman Brothers, which was hitting all-time highs with its rapidly expanding business. This growth required increased networking capabilities, and Lehman Brothers sought out the new start-up because of its promising technology. But as fate would have it, Lehman Brothers would go on to file for bankruptcy only a month later.

Arastra's flagship customer and all its future revenues evaporated. A false start, but one that teased at the potential of this start-up business. Our CEO sensed that the setback was only temporary. The technology it produced was market-leading and too good to be ignored forever. She also felt she belonged. The team of senior leaders consisted of people she had known and respected, and they too recognised her efforts and abilities. She was motivated to succeed for them as much as for herself. In due course, she would also be rewarded handsomely if she could generate long-term growth. And as it turned out over the 16 years that followed, she became a billionaire as a result of the 3 per cent ownership she accumulated via the stock options she received as part of her pay package.

Under her leadership, Arastra was renamed to Arista Networks and began a carefully planned international expansion. It targeted highly strategic entry points — that being high-end customers, typically in financial services and media, who required the fastest and most advanced networking solutions on the market. Over time, the melding of hardware and software has given Arista prime position in advanced fields such as artificial intelligence (AI) that require Arista's high-bandwidth network technology.

As at time of writing, Jayshree Ullal still remains as Arista's CEO — one of the longest-serving CEOs in Silicon Valley and one of only a handful of females from an ethnic minority background. Highly revered and influential, Ullal holds immense power as the products developed by Arista underpin much of the advanced developments we are seeing in technology today. She has been celebrated for leading Arista through its IPO in 2014 and its journey to being a US$100 billion company that generated US$6 billion in sales in 2023. She has been vocal in Arista's rivalry with her former employer Cisco. In some ways it has motivated her to chase the dream of overtaking Cisco and leaving her mark on the industry. She continues to work with Andy Bechtolsheim, the co-founder of Arista Networks and its majority shareholder, who is the former colleague who reached out to her with a job offer in 2008. Even though she did not start out as an owner, the traits demonstrated by Ullal and the outcomes of psychological ownership are evident through her behaviours and the results she has delivered for Arista and its shareholders. Already a billionaire, what keeps her motivated is more than just a large salary and bonuses — it is a deeper motivator from within.

This executive's career demonstrates the perfect balance of extrinsic and intrinsic motivators at play, unlocking the hidden superpower of psychological ownership, and achieving absolute alignment between the individual and an organisation.

PART II: RECAP

How aligned is management with shareholders (and the board)?

◆ All executive managers have great experience and expertise. What separates effective teams is their motivation and how aligned they are with the owners of the company.

◆ Motivations run deeper than just financial incentives. Start with assessing the intrinsic motivators of autonomy, mastery, and purpose when evaluating an executive management team and consider how these motivators are being harnessed.

◆ Situations where already-wealthy executives take on modest pay packets are favourable.

◆ Keep an eye on executives who like the limelight. Is their media prominence furthering the brand of the company? Or is it only beneficial to the executive?

◆ Look for remuneration structures where cash is kept to a minimum and long-term incentives make up the bulk of compensation packages.

◆ Executives that become fixated on financial rewards will be less motivated by long-term drivers. Look for maximum limits on the levels of the financial incentives on offer.

◆ Long deferral periods allow time for results to show — it is a good sign to see when executives delay their payoff longer than the usual timeframe. At least five years is ideal.

- Remuneration packages with a long deferral period and outsized equity-linked rewards encourage executives to make bold decisions.

- A large portion of key performance indicator (KPI) metrics should be focused on building the reputation and 'brand' of the company. The test is: If the management team leaves, will the effects of these brand building initiatives remain enduring with the company?

- Look at the behaviours of executive team members and whether psychological ownership has been unlocked — this is the indicator for maximum alignment. What frameworks and policies are in place to build engagement and target the various categories of extrinsic and intrinsic motivators?

- Long-term-focused founder-led companies exhibit a strong alignment between management, board, and shareholders.

PART III
Influence

*'Influence is not the power to change minds, but the
ability to change hearts.'*

— **Anonymous**

The concept of influence in leadership has been written and talked about ad nauseam. However, much of this discussion focuses on influence at the individual level—how a single leader, person, or protagonist influences another to achieve a desired outcome. This part of the book shifts focus to the influence exerted by the management team, rather than individual executives. From a business success perspective, the significance of influence lies in the management team's ability to spread the company's philosophy and vision throughout the organisation and to its customers.

In this part, I present the Influence Scorecard, a systematic approach to evaluating management's capacity to lead and inspire. The resulting score serves as a key indicator of a management team's effectiveness in the *influence* pillar of the Founder Framework—measuring how successfully executives can motivate employees to achieve strategic objectives and, in turn, persuade customers to engage with the brand and its offerings. How adept are they at commanding the masses?

The Influence Scorecard (figure P3-1, overleaf) breaks down management's influence into two components: first, how well they leverage their internal workforce, and second, how effective they are at attracting a radical base externally.

Influence Scorecard

INTERNAL		EXTERNAL	
Proximity to Customers	/ 10	Uniqueness	/ 10
Distributed Autonomy	/ 10	Building a Movement	/ 10
Total Score	/ 40		

Figure P3-1: The Influence Scorecard.

Crucially, both components are visible to external observers. Instead of getting bogged down by the complexities of organisational reporting lines to determine influence, we focus on fundamental principles. For a management team to be truly influential, it must structure the organisation in a way that amplifies its message. At the same time, it must guard against the cognitive biases that inevitably arise as the company grows. When management turns its attention outwards to engage with customers, it can influence purchasing decisions only by presenting a distinctive value proposition and aligning the brand with current societal trends and customer values.

Let me begin with the story of one of the world's largest brands — a tale of redemption and revival. It illustrates how decades of built influence was lost when management failed to adapt to shifting societal trends, but was ultimately regained when, after some deep reflection, it rediscovered both its influence over its internal workforce and its ability to ingeniously captivate a new audience.

Influence rediscovered

Leg godt. These two Danish words translate directly as 'play well' — a simple and powerful philosophy that has guided the LEGO Group since its founding in 1932. The genesis of LEGO was more a product of happenstance rather than any sophisticated planning. In fact, LEGO's founder, Ole Kirk Kristiansen, had fallen into making children's toys as they proved more affordable and therefore easier to sell amid the Great Depression. The economic downturn had put immense pressure on his fledgling carpentry business, which started out selling ladders, ironing boards, and other household products. The crisis had forced Kristiansen to examine his company closely; after a period of trial and error, he decided to pivot into yo-yos, wooden ducks, and toy trucks. His move came despite opposition from his siblings, with whom he had taken out an emergency loan.[1] His stubbornness was the source of his trademark perseverance — a characteristic that has led to what is now the world's most reputable company[2] and each year generates over US$1.8 billion of net profit.[3] Remarkably, the company is still 100 per cent controlled by Kristiansen's family and the family's philanthropic foundation.

I have only shared how LEGO started and what it looks like now. What I have not covered is the difficult period in the early 2000s in which LEGO's management team faced intensifying competition as its patent expired, combined with a rise in video games, which took children's attention away from physical toys. This led to a period of what many thought was the start of LEGO's demise.[4] The strategies that have been well executed by LEGO's management team since those dark days demonstrate how harnessing influence can dramatically change a company's fortunes.

In 2004, LEGO's CEO and owner, Kjeld Kirk Kristiansen (the grandson of the founder) was stepping down. He had led the company for 25 years, overseeing a golden age of growth that had eventually stagnated, leading to a period of uncertainty and loss-making by the time he announced his departure. His replacement was to be the 35-year-old Director of Strategy Jørgen Vig Knudstorp, who had never been in charge of a company, let alone one as large as LEGO. But Kristiansen, being the owner, saw something special in his pick and, importantly, had the final say. With the family fortune on the line, he was prepared to back this promising young leader.

To give you a sense of how dire the situation was, the incoming Knudstorp recalls, 'Had the company not been owned by a wealthy private family, it would have been technically insolvent.'[5] And it was against this backdrop that Knudstorp stepped forward into the spotlight, choosing to strip back the company to first principles before rebuilding it again.

LEGO had grown too bureaucratic and complacent. Its organisational structure had become too rigid and hierarchical, to the point of being blinded by its past success. To change the *thinking* of the company, and for management to have any chance of internal influence, Knudstorp had to first restructure it. He streamlined business units and reallocated bloated teams as quickly as he could. He also put in tighter financial controls to stem the immediate bleeding.

After the restructure was complete, the management team knew it had to influence and reshape the organisation's mindset. But to what? What mindset was required to reignite growth? In the past, LEGO had been too focused on the numbers — sales figures, the number of product launches, the number of collaborations, store openings. Knudstorp knew this fixation was the output LEGO would need to aim for, but that it missed the real heart of solving the immediate issue. It wasn't about the numbers. That was too clinical; here were businesspeople in suits with fancy presentations, projections, and performance metrics trying to sell plastic building blocks to infants, toddlers, and children. Knudstorp knew the solution had to be about the *feeling* the LEGO brand engendered in its employees and target audience — its internal organisation and the broader audience of young families. If the management team could get that right, the numbers would follow.

He began seeking answers internally from his employees first:[5]

◆   'What does it mean to work at LEGO?'

◆   'What's our unique proposition for our retail customers, families, and kids?'

◆   'What are the values that we really like?'

Though he had a sense of direction, he understood these were not questions for him or the management team to dictate. To wield real influence, it could not be imposed from above like a royal decree; instead, it needed to arise organically from his employees and customers. The answers to these questions were key to unlocking LEGO's influence again. And with the financial backing that is only possible from a patient long-term shareholder, the management team was able to deploy significant capital and resources to ask those fundamental questions to employees and customers through an extensive global research project. The insights the team uncovered from this research would shape LEGO's interactions with customers for the next two decades and catapult it back to the top of the world's leading brands.

The first insight was how the act of playing had changed over the years. In order for LEGO to keep up, it had to tie itself closely to the art of play. Creative Director Søren Holm recalled a particular focus group: 'We asked an 11-year-old German boy, "what is your favourite possession?" And he pointed to his shoes. When we asked him why these were so important to him, he showed us how they were worn on the side and bottom.' The boy explained that the sneakers' wear-and-tear showed that he had mastered a difficult skateboarding trick, one that had taken him 'hours and hours to perfect'.[5] In other words, children valued play that challenged them. They were motivated by achievement, whereas LEGO sets had become too easy and too prescriptive in how they should be assembled.

Harness their intrinsic motivation. Video games, one of the competitors to physical play, were adept at tapping into this motivator with level progressions and unlocking new abilities as players became more skilful. The management team returned to the drawing board, expanding the concept of play to include programming and STEM (science, technology, engineering, mathematics) disciplines. It introduced LEGO sets that could be controlled through software and coding, offering players the freedom to code as they wished and engage at different levels of complexity. This was a deliberate effort to preserve the essence of physical play, the core of the LEGO brand, while integrating digital elements like apps, digital controls, and video games. Global research underscored LEGO's strength in the physical realm — its true differentiator — something video games could never replicate. And so, LEGO leaned into this unique advantage.

The second big revelation was the power of digital reach. With kids spending more time on mobile devices and gaming, LEGO was losing touchpoints to influence its core audience. But this also presented an opportunity to meet them where they were — on the very platforms they were glued to. Management decided to ramp up efforts in social media, gaming, and collaborations to maximise customer engagement.

But before LEGO could conquer the digital world, it had to get its own house in order. The entire digital strategy, including backend systems, needed a serious overhaul. Everything was interconnected — customer relationship management, marketing, supply chain, HR, planning, and internal communications. Knudstorp and his team learned a vital lesson: To effectively influence customers, they first had to ensure their internal systems were rock solid. Strengthening influence with employees through better communication and streamlined backend processes was key to making the company-wide changes flow to the front lines.

And so, LEGO reorganised itself — both digitally and hierarchically.[4] Once the internal transformation was complete, influencing customers became a much smoother process.

The third key insight was the power of community. LEGO needed to revive its brand, restoring the cult-like status it enjoyed in the 1970s and 1980s, making the LEGO name synonymous with the art of play. To do this, management accelerated partnerships with the film and television industries, producing movies and LEGO-building competitions that showcased the endless creative potential of the iconic building block. The objective was to engender a cult army of LEGO enthusiasts that would be brand fanatics.

Next, LEGO embraced inclusivity, introducing LEGO Braille Bricks and launching campaigns like 'Ready for Girls' and 'Play Is Your Superpower'. It even appealed to adults with its architecture line, allowing them to recreate the world's most iconic buildings.

LEGO's journey has spanned over two decades, starting with a desperate need to stop the bleeding, followed by a bold reinvention. Since those bleak days, LEGO has increased its revenue tenfold and never looked back (see figure P3-2). Despite the rise of mobile devices and console games, both kids and adults still gravitate toward LEGO sets. Through a well-executed strategy, the management team has not only won over customers but also unlocked the full potential of LEGO's employees.

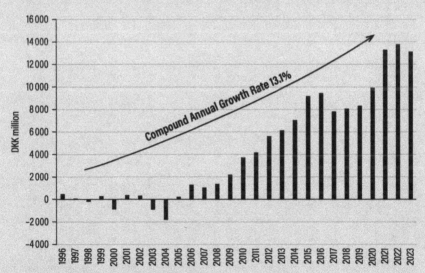

Figure P3-2: LEGO's net profit, 1996–2023.

LEGO's success is not as elusive as it may seem. In chapters 6 and 7, I will explore each aspect of the Influence Scorecard in detail, guiding you in recognising the traits of a truly influential management team. We begin by examining how we can gain insight into a company's inner workings from an external perspective.

CHAPTER 6

Internal influence: Leveraging the workforce

What drives true value creation is the influence of the executive management team as a unit—its ability to compel employees to go the extra mile—so a key factor in influencing employees lies in the structure of the organisation. Management cannot rely solely on positional power to drive action—it is not a dictatorship. While command-and-control might work in the military, business is a different game, where success depends on winning over customers, not just issuing orders. For this to happen, employees must be inspired to align with the executive team's goals. This is only achievable when the organisational structure fosters, rather than obstructs, a two-way flow of influence between management, employees, and customers (see figure 6-1, overleaf). Just as management needs to effectively communicate strategic objectives internally, the two-way flow of influence allows management to stay closely attuned to customers, keeping an eye on shifting preferences and emerging opportunities.

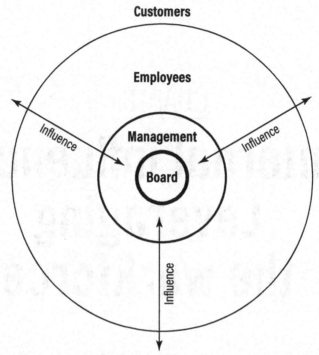

Figure 6-1: The circle of influence is a two-way flow.

In this chapter, we examine the internal influence rating, which measures a management team's capacity to effectively extend its influence across the organisation, forming the first half of the comprehensive Influence Scorecard. For external observers, our assessment focuses on identifying key attributes within the organisational infrastructure that enable effective influence. Much like LEGO's management had to first address its internal organisational structure before regaining its influence, we must also start by examining how the organisation is structured. If we imagine influence as a flow of electricity, organisational design is the layout of the company's power grid with which executive management sends its instructions and signals. If the power grid is well laid out, the signals that management generates are transmitted efficiently and accurately internally, and its signage and lights on the outside of the building will shine brightly, attracting attention from customers. However, if the power grid is too convoluted or inefficient, the signal becomes muddled; the outside signage and lights will not work properly. If there are no feedback loops built in, management cannot even rectify this issue as it has no avenue to receive feedback from the outside world. Management's ability to influence its teams and its target customers becomes restricted. As outsiders, we are looking for organisational structures that keep management in close proximity to customers, not ones that become bureaucratic and inefficient, like government institutions.

Maintaining proximity to customers

As an organisation expands to thousands, and eventually tens of thousands of employees, it is almost inevitable that its structure will grow to encompass multiple hierarchical layers. Several rapidly growing Australian superannuation (pension) funds, for instance, now employ over 500 staff with organisational structures spanning eight layers, from the board down to client engagement. A major Australian gambling company, with over 30000 employees, follows a similar model with eight layers between the board and the front line.

With so many layers for messages to traverse—where information can easily get lost or distorted—how can organisations ensure that the essence of executive communications reaches those on the ground, intact? To wield real influence, executives must have a steady flow of up-to-date insights into every level of the organisation. But here is the intriguing part: As outsiders, we can spot the telltale signs of whether management is truly engaged and nurturing a genuine, two-way connection, or if it is simply corporate rhetoric. Several objective indicators can guide us in this assessment.

Minimising layers

The optimal organisational design keeps hierarchical layers to the bare minimum. The appropriate number of layers will depend on the nature of the business. What outsiders need to spot is an excessive number of layers that 'distance' key decision-makers from end customers.

If you have insider connections with employees, ask them how many layers of hierarchy stretch from the front lines to the top executives. Find out if each layer has clear responsibilities, or if there is a bunch of middle management that seems to be just floating without real accountability or decision-making power. Take a retailer, for example—typically, you will see geographic divisions that outline responsibilities from the store level up through districts, states, and country. Ideally, there should be just a few more layers before you hit the executive level; otherwise, you are staring down the barrel of a bureaucratic nightmare with too many layers to manage effectively.

Be wary of large corporations with towering, pyramid-like structures—the bigger the company, the more layers it tends to pile on. Financial institutions like banks and insurers are classic examples of these traditional setups. Ask a bank employee about the levels in their organisation's hierarchy, and they might only be able to name a few of the layers above them without peeking at the organisation chart. Some of Australia's largest banks, with their 30 000+ staff, have up to nine layers separating their boards from their retail teams.

As companies grow and evolve, they often add more people and layers, creating an ivory tower effect where management becomes increasingly detached from the customer-facing teams—and, ultimately, from the customers themselves. Overlayered structures go against the notion of fluid knowledge and information flows. Senior executive teams might receive a crucial message, but by the time it reaches them it can easily become garbled, so the true issue is completely lost within the layers through interpretation and re-articulation.

Information is influence

At the bedrock of the psychology behind influence lies current and accurate information. Information is what facilitates the ability to apply the foundational principles of influence (for example, to utilise empathy and understand others). For an executive team to influence effectively, it must always have an accurate sense of the 'cultural temperature' of its organisational teams, as well as of customer sentiment. ('Cultural temperature' is not an academically supported phrase, just a term I found quite fitting when I heard it in the HBO series *Succession*—it essentially refers to the employee sentiment and overall vibe towards a company.) From an internal sense, this is different to gleaning employee engagement through the usual annual engagement surveys, which are focused on a point in time and which organisations tend to be relatively slow to garner insight from (or to act upon any issues identified).

As outsiders, we are unlikely to have access to this level of granular detail, nor is it necessary. Anecdotal evidence is subjective and does not tell us about the holistic picture throughout the organisation. For this reason, we should focus on objective information based on the fundamental setup of the company.

A definitive way to assess whether a business maintains effective information flow to its executive teams is to directly inquire during opportunities such as Annual General Meetings. While shareholders typically concentrate on financial matters, questions like, 'How do you ensure that this project or strategy has the support of all team members at every level?' can reveal much about the organisation's communication practices. To gain a clearer picture of internal operations and their effectiveness, consider asking:

- What systems are in place to ensure that the voices of all employees and customers are consistently integrated into decision-making?

- How frequently are executive leaders engaged with front-line teams and customers?

- What procedures exist for teams to provide feedback and raise concerns, and how is this feedback addressed?

These questions target the frameworks, policies, and programs established to maintain effective information flow—the organisational setup—rather than transient events or anecdotal employee experiences. The answers will reveal whether the organisation is truly dedicated to nurturing open communication or merely adopting superficial measures.

Allow me to illustrate an approach to organisational setup that both minimises layers between executives and customers and naturally promotes two-way information flow. This innovative structure, which taps into our primal instincts, was employed by an iconoclastic CEO and founder I had the pleasure of meeting.[1,2]

Close to the ground: A tribal approach

From its humble beginnings with a single retail store in 1982, Flight Centre Travel Group has soared to become a global travel conglomerate, boasting a market value of US$3.1 billion and annual revenues of US$2 billion. Graham Turner, the visionary founder and CEO, has always rejected conventional hierarchies. Instead, he has pioneered an approach that keeps executives directly connected to customers — a critical strategy given the company's diverse clientele. His rationale? Being close to the customer accelerates decision-making, cuts through bureaucracy, and maintains a dynamic feedback loop between clients and management — key elements for wielding true *influence*.

Flight Centre's rapid growth has been fuelled by insights from evolutionary psychology, specifically the work of Professor Nigel Nicholson from the London School of Economics. Graham Turner harnessed these insights from our fundamental human instincts and applied them to his business. He adopted a 'tribes' approach, tapping into our deep-rooted need for connection. This strategy mirrors our natural drive for family bonds and social ties, where loyalty, connection, and shared values forge a strong community.[3] Just as families are the building blocks of our social fabric, multiple families unite to form networks, villages, and ultimately tribes, with shared goals and values.

Evolutionary psychology suggests humans can maintain meaningful relationships in groups of up to 150, a concept known as *Dunbar's number* (derived from the well-known research conducted by Robin Dunbar, which asserts there is a cognitive limit to the number of people with whom humans are able to maintain social relationships). For smaller companies, this works well, but as Flight Centre grew into the hundreds and thousands, staying connected to customer needs became increasingly difficult as more employees were added to the organisation chart. To overcome this, Turner and the executive team introduced a scalable structure that tackled the challenge of Dunbar's number while allowing the management team to expand this business rapidly. Turner's tribe-based approach, designed to keep teams tightly knit and agile, proved so effective that Flight Centre continues to use it to this day.

The organisational design centres around small, bonded teams of five to eight people—a model that mirrors the way our hunter-gatherer ancestors thrived in tight-knit families. Just as five to eight people formed families in the past, Turner applies this concept to Flight Centre, with each retail shop functioning as a 'family'. As each shop grows, instead of adding more people, Flight Centre chooses to open new, nearby shops. Running contrary to the popular economies-of-scale argument, Turner's approach has proven far more effective as it counters the social loafing effect and ignites an entrepreneurial spirit by providing autonomy to each family.

Clusters of three to five shops are grouped into 'villages', with 25 to 40 people collaborating, sharing resources, and supporting each other. The true innovation comes in the form of 'tribes'—consisting of three to five villages, or 20 to 30 families, within a region. Each tribe operates as its own profit centre, with its own internal name, branding, and a culture of healthy competition at company events. With around 80 to 150 members, these tribes allow leaders to maintain close relationships with their teams and stay connected to daily operations. Rather than having state-based divisions, each tribe leader shares in the tribe's profits, functioning as a partner or owner, effectively running their own Flight Centre business within their jurisdiction.[4]

Beyond the tribe level, there are only two additional layers—country and global—ensuring that the executive team remained closely connected to its customers (see figure 6-2). As customer demand grows, new families, villages, and tribes are formed, creating a scalable and dynamic system. By capping the size of each layer, Turner's structure aligns with our inherent human desire for community, enabling smoother communication between management, employees, and customers.

At first glance, the internal workings of an organisation's structure might seem like information hidden from outsiders. However, in the case of Flight Centre, this is not the case. Companies that take pride in their innovative approaches often share these details openly to

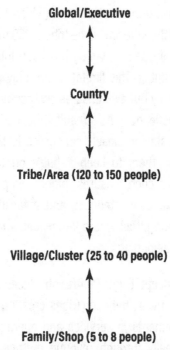

Figure 6-2: The organisation structure at Flight Centre.

distinguish themselves from the conventional model. Flight Centre, for example, publicly outlines its tribe-based structure on its website and annual reports.

From an outsider's perspective, Flight Centre's organisational design aligns with its customer-centric focus. After all, a travel agency's success is inextricably linked to its ability to deliver a delightful customer experience. In arranging its structure in such a way, Flight Centre's customer-facing team members remain two layers away from the tribe leader, who has direct accountability for the growth and welfare of their tribe. Tribe leaders remain close to the customer (by having full access to regular customer surveys and tribe reports) and, since they have the responsibility of an owner of their tribe, they have both the authority and motivation to implement new initiatives as their customer base evolves. Executives remain within five layers of front-line staff.

Unlike traditional hierarchical structures (which place no cap on the size of a group), Flight Centre limits one tribe to 150 members and families of no more than eight people, which has been intentionally designed around Dunbar's number. This limitation not only prevents the rise of excessive bureaucracy but also ensures swift communication from the front line to the tribe leaders. As a result, tribe leaders are incentivised to act like owners, staying closely connected to both employees and customers, allowing them to keep a pulse on the business's daily dynamics. This approach ensures higher employee engagement, promoting employee connectedness and a feeling of being valued, avoiding the common pitfall where larger teams lead to a diminished sense of individual belonging.

Building on this concept, Flight Centre introduces extrinsic motivators by fostering friendly rivalry between tribes, creating competitive tension that drives improvements in services and operations. Competition is fostered both formally through revenue metrics and rankings, and informally through staff conferences, where tribes go head-to-head in challenges and dress-up contests. The notion of a tribe is quite literal as tribes come up with their own names to distinguish themselves and stand out. The goal of these initiatives is to foster a fun company culture that taps into our innate need for belonging. The internal friendly competition is designed to take away complacency and promote entrepreneurism, in much the same way as we would see businesses compete within a large city, which in turn encourages differentiation and therefore productivity gains.

Dividing a big company into smaller pieces is how large organisations can improve productivity per employee and continue to harness the inherent desire of humans to feel like they can make a meaningful contribution through their work. Flight Centre's organisation structure allows it to scale up or down depending on customer demand by forming new shops (families), villages, and tribes when required, while struggling tribes will naturally succumb to Darwin's law of evolution and natural selection (effectively, survival of the fittest) and be reallocated to other areas of the business.

Flight Centre continues to be structured as tribes — a way of organising a company that is ingrained in the culture of the business. Furthermore, Graham Turner remains adamant that the size of its board and senior management team should be no different than a family — a maximum of five to eight people — in 2024, Flight Centre had six board members, six C-suite executives, and three regional heads, which oversee 15 000 employees across the entire group. The rationale? To streamline the flow of information directly to executives and allow them to stay intimately connected with customers' evolving needs and desires.

Structures that distribute autonomy

Great management teams that lead by influence have a knack for sparking the entrepreneurial spirit in their workforce. Influence, by nature, is not a one-way street. It is more like a gentle nudge, a subtle push that guides employees toward the strategic goals set by the executive team. To inspire people to go the extra mile, there needs to be room for creative freedom in how they execute the overall strategy. As organisations grow, executives have less direct contact with every employee, so they must find ways to embed their philosophy and strategy without micromanaging every step.

Think of the most rigid organisations you have come across — probably ones with endless checklists and procedures that turn employees into glorified box-tickers, right? (Did government departments come to mind?) This kind of prescriptive setup leaves no space for proactive thinking, innovation, or initiative.

As external observers, we are testing for the executive team's ability to delegate the execution of its objectives. At one end of the spectrum, there is the strict, authoritarian style that dictates exactly how strategies should be carried out. At the other end, you have the outcomes-focused teams that set big-picture goals and give others the freedom to figure out how to achieve them. The authoritarian approach hoards autonomy at the top, while the outcomes-focused method spreads it throughout the company. The best management teams actively look for ways to distribute autonomy, creating clear structures where power is delegated and responsibilities are well defined. Effective leadership and influence do not come from dictating to a workforce, but from setting clear boundaries and giving people the freedom to achieve their goals. The most effective way to foster this autonomy is through an organisational structure built to support this approach.

As discussed in the example 'Close to the ground: A tribal approach', Graham Turner's 'tribes' approach at Flight Centre not only keeps the executive team closely connected to customers, but also sparks entrepreneurial energy within each tribe. This structure is one way to distribute autonomy—though it is not the only way to achieve it.

As outsiders, once you know what to look for, these structures become easy to spot. The more you observe from a global perspective, the sharper your eye will become at recognising them. Let me show you what distributed autonomy can look like through a few different examples.

The centralised conglomerate

Louis Vuitton Moët Hennessy (LVMH), a vast luxury conglomerate with over 196 000 employees from more than 190 nationalities, has mastered the art of maintaining lean and agile decision-making despite its immense scale. At the heart of its centralised structure is the philosophy of granting as much autonomy as possible to its subsidiaries, allowing each to develop bespoke business strategies tailored to their specific target markets. CEO and Chairman Bernard Arnault, alongside his leadership team, retains authority only over critical group-wide decisions, such as identifying and acquiring target companies. Beyond these strategic choices, the 75 individual brands within the group, known as *maisons*, are empowered to pursue their own growth strategies and are held accountable for generating profit with minimal intervention from Arnault and his team.

LVMH achieves cohesion across its decentralised maisons through a select number of shared divisions that provide essential services, including finance and legal support, ensuring compliance, risk management, and sustainability initiatives. The group's LIFE (LVMH Initiatives for the Environment) program centralises sustainability efforts and reporting across all maisons.

This approach captures the essence of breaking a large company into smaller, agile units, allowing them to stay deeply connected while operating independently with greater autonomy. LVMH's organisational structure is a prime example, perfectly tailored to the luxury sector. Each maison preserves its distinct identity and strategic freedom to cater to its specific customer base, striking a balance between scalability and focus. By distributing its 196 000 employees across independent maisons, LVMH ensures that every brand remains close to its customers while maintaining a high level of flexibility.

(As an aside, Bernard Arnault, although not technically the founder of LVMH, took control and has been the guiding visionary behind the company's strategy since 1989.[5] How he came into power at LVMH is a fascinating story of how a young man was able to outmanoeuvre two seasoned executives.)

Other companies have adopted a centralised conglomerate structure successfully, including Warren Buffett's Berkshire Hathaway and the under-the-radar Swedish company Lifco, which specialises in acquiring niche companies in dental, demolition and tools, and system solutions businesses. Lifco's approach is similar to Berkshire Hathaway's — it acquires private businesses and rolls them into Lifco's publicly listed structure, which then creates liquidity and synergy for the whole group of companies. Each company sits under the Lifco umbrella, operating with individual targets while benefiting from the shared resources and services of a larger group. Reply SpA, covered in Chapter 2, segments its teams into specialised boutique companies, each dedicated to a specific service line and geographic region. While these boutiques operate independently, they maintain a centralised structure, with key decisions governed by the head office and shared services like accounting and finance. This model closely mirrors the approach used by LVMH.

Companies with a centralised conglomerate structure tend to get the right level of distributed autonomy, encouraging their subsidiaries to stay entrepreneurial and accountable for their own success, while a central management team keeps everything aligned and handles big-picture decisions. It is not the only way to organise a company, but it taps into our tribal instincts. As humans, we crave simplicity in team dynamics — clear responsibilities, a sense of psychological ownership, and enough proximity to senior management that they know who can step in when needed.

For outsiders, spotting a structure that effectively distributes autonomy is key. Look for companies that break down their workforce into smaller groups that fit within Dunbar's number. This is usually easy to find in annual reports or on corporate websites. Companies with innovative structures are unafraid to showcase them, and for good reason. Take Flight Centre, LVMH, and Reply SpA—these companies unashamedly announce their unique distributed structure publicly on their websites and in investor documents. These executive teams confidently signal their interpretation of how businesses should be run; they are masters at leveraging their workforce.

Before you assume this model is universally replicable, let me share the intriguing story of an ambitious American company that made a bold attempt at distributing autonomy. While the company ultimately did not succeed, the lessons from its experience reveal the fine line between an effective distribution of autonomy and one that lacks the guiding hand of leadership—the company stumbled because one crucial principle was overlooked.

Learnings from a failed experiment in autonomy

In 2013, online shoe retailer Zappos announced it was undertaking a significant change in the way it would operate.[6] At the time, the US-based company was already on the way to becoming the next up-and-coming ecommerce player. It had grown from a start-up to over 1500 employees in a short period of time. And much the same as an adolescent in need of new clothes, Zappos needed to rethink how it reorganised itself for its next phase of growth.

The management team had come across Edward Glaeser's research in his book *Triumph of the City* and was inspired by one of his enlightening discoveries: Whenever a city doubles in size, each resident's productivity increases 15 per cent.[7] This ran counter to the experience of most businesses, which usually suffer from the headwinds of size – the productivity of each employee diminishes as more people are hired – a factor often overlooked and chalked down to corporate bureaucracy.

Certainly, Zappos was no different — it had itself experienced diminishing productivity returns for each employee it hired.

Led by a determined founder, the management team at Zappos was loathe to sit idly and accept that it was just another company plagued with the same issue. It was in a growth phase; it was critical for the company to maintain momentum while also maintaining its uniquely high level of employee and customer engagement. This meant trying a radically different approach when it came to redesigning its company structure. The executive team was determined to solve the pertinent question that Glaeser's research raised: Why is it that cities can build momentum through size, but companies become less effective as they get bigger?

Earlier that year Zappos had already embarked on the bold move of its headquarters from Henderson to downtown Las Vegas. The move had a well-considered rationale of improving staff engagement and accessing a new pool of contact centre workers. Amid these upgrades, management noticed decisions were taking longer to make. For example, more approvals were needed when a change in course was required which, at a time when plenty of changes were needed, proved to be a hindrance to Zappos' growth ambitions. A redesign was also on the cards, but what shape it would take was unclear.

There was one key influence that would determine the future direction of Zappos. First, the company had been shaped by its upbringing — the founder had created its success through an unwavering focus on employee and customer satisfaction. It was the very reason why it did not outsource its contact centre overseas — the management team did not believe in giving up its core competencies, so it wanted to retain what differentiated Zappos from other online businesses. This underlying philosophy would remain key to any future redesign. Customer engagement was essential, so it decided to try and run its business in the same way a city is structured and run, rather than relying on traditional corporate hierarchies. This meant forgoing the hierarchical pyramid in favour of a new, flexible, adaptable approach that encouraged employees to self-manage — much like how the residents of a city would organise themselves. This was why the idea of self-management first entered the boardroom discussion at Zappos.

For context, the concept of *self-management* is not a new one. It was first observed in the 1950s when coal miners in South Yorkshire, England, began adopting a structure that went against 'longwall' mining, which was the prevailing way of working. The traditional longwall mining approach was widely accepted as best practice and borrowed heavily from Henry Ford's assembly line principles — each team performed a single task, and each task was completed sequentially. Longwall mining meant the workflow was extremely reliable but not very adaptable.

Then some miners decided to adopt their own approach in South Yorkshire — a totally different approach, and the first recorded observation of self-management. Rather than following a traditional conveyor-belt-style workflow, independent teams were created, each equipped with diverse skill sets, enabling them to switch roles and shifts with minimal oversight. This more flexible, non-linear approach significantly enhanced productivity, as teams could operate around the clock without being delayed by other groups — an issue often seen with the longwall method. This self-management model defied the conventional wisdom of the time, which held that task repetition was the key to greater efficiency and productivity. It also appealed to workers as they felt more engaged with this newfound autonomy and the opportunity to develop multiple skills by working across different roles.

As self-management evolved into the 1970s and 1980s, a growing number of companies carved out divisions that would operate under the philosophy. In Europe, it became known as *industrial democracy* and in Japan the concept was taken further through the principle of *kaizen* or *continuous improvement*, whereby the people closest to the task were empowered to implement incremental improvements. The Volvo plant in Kalmar, Sweden, reduced defects by 90 per cent in 1987. FedEx cut service errors by 13 per cent in 1989. In the late 1980s and early 1990s, C&S Wholesale Grocers created a warehouse of self-managed teams, which enjoyed a 60 per cent cost advantage over competitors, and General Mills increased productivity by up to 40 per cent in plants that adopted self-managed teams.[8] The most significant gains were found in manufacturing and service operation divisions, which were traditionally organised in more rigid structures and benefited from the adaptability self-management offered. Due to the success in these discrete divisions, the application of self-management began expanding into broader areas by fast-growing companies as the internet economy took hold and, although the jargon changed, the principles remained much the same. For example, the use of agile and scrum methodologies in today's world harks back to the ideology that tasks can be broken up into small pieces, which different teams tackle and iterate quickly to solve, while avoiding being bogged down by over-planning.

Forward-thinking companies were increasingly seeking to ingrain the self-management approach throughout the entire business rather than just in discrete divisions. And so in 2007, Brian Robertson, a former programmer, came up with *holacracy*, a system of organising teams with the core tenet of distributed authority. In essence, an entire company could be broken down into small teams with no traditional management layer (see figure 6-3). It worked well for software development companies, so Zappos was keen to see if it could work for them.

Just as a city operates without rigid hierarchies, Zappos would eschew traditional structures (see figure 6-4) in favour of super circles and sub-circles, where staff would be organised into collaborative teams, each with its own authority. The conventional layers would be replaced by these teams, which function like micro-economies within a larger organisation.

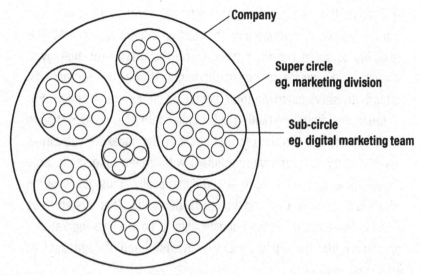

Figure 6-3: A holacratic organisation structure.

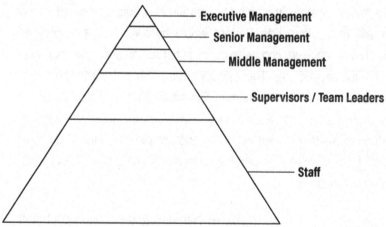

Figure 6-4: Traditional hierarchical organisation structure.

To use the city analogy, imagine a restaurant economy with diverse eateries, surrounded by essential services such as cleaning, supply, and waste management, each operating as sub-teams within the broader framework. This approach mirrors the dynamic, interconnected nature of a city, fostering a more flexible and integrated organisational structure.

At Zappos, 150 traditional departments were transformed into 500 sub-circles, each operating with relative independence and the flexibility to serve various circles. Using the restaurant analogy, a sub-circle like waste management might, during quieter periods, extend its services to another sector, such as construction. For instance, the digital marketing sub-circle could offer its expertise to other circles, such as the product circle or the sneakers sub-circle. Just as a city becomes more efficient with growth and reallocates resources as needed, Zappos would dynamically adjust its resource allocation to meet evolving business demands. This system was designed to function autonomously, akin to how a free-market city operates under the guidance of the invisible hand of capitalism. At least, that was the vision.

At Zappos, the application of holacracy involved the creation of a free market system in which staff resources would be ranked based on skill rather than title. Badges would be awarded for employees that have achieved competence in a particular area (for example, marketing copywriting). These badges could only be awarded by senior employees, who acted as mentors. The more badges one could acquire, the more senior and valuable they would become under this system. Following the free market approach, each employee would likely be in multiple sub-circles and therefore tasked with using their skills across different functions.

To diverge further from traditional hierarchies, the allocation of staff would be determined by 'people points' — each super circle would be given a certain number of points for recruiting internal staff, and each staff member could accept or join another super circle — this effectively created a marketplace for human resources. The total number of people points allocated to each super circle would be determined by senior management's assessment of the value of each super circle.

There were two major implications of the people points system, both of which would have adverse ramifications later down the track. These were:

1. Employees could be leaders in some circles but not in others. This was because employees could have multiple roles across different super circles.

2. Each Zappos employee had 7.4 roles on average.

It was clear from the outset that holacracy would be a major shift from traditional structures, requiring extensive training to reshape employees' mindsets. Further, due to the multiple roles each employee was accountable for, they experienced a diminishing rate of productivity per employee. Internal reviews confirmed employee productivity declined with each additional role, supported by psychological research on goal setting. People are more productive with a focused set of tasks; too many responsibilities lead to mental switching costs — a draining effect caused by excessive multitasking.[9]

By 2020, seven years after Zappos adopted holacracy, the company had significantly evolved from its initial textbook model. This was not due to a lack of effort, but rather a series of adjustments needed to keep the system functioning effectively and enhance employee productivity. The changes grew increasingly complex, contrary to the principle of simplicity and creating confusion. Human nature craves clarity and simplicity in task assignment; we often associate leadership with accountability, much like villagers look to elders for guidance. Self-managed organisations challenge this instinct, as individuals may be leaders in one context but followers in another — much like a village elder who is a chief for some tasks and a subordinate for others. At Zappos, this complexity left employees unsure whether to adhere to the new system based on their roles or to follow the directives of their previous managers.

Although Zappos fell short in its attempt to emulate the dynamic nature of cities, there were positive takeaways. The Zappos experience highlights the benefits of a flexible approach to roles, where employees were encouraged to develop skills across multiple disciplines, enhancing both their seniority and value to the company. This structure taps into our intrinsic motivators and allows executives to distribute autonomy. Rather than confining individuals to fixed positions, Zappos embraced internal mobility, allowing for dynamic resource allocation as needed. Furthermore, the shift toward smaller, more agile teams is a positive strategy, akin to Flight Centre's approach and the inherent adaptability seen in cities, where fluid structures drive efficiency and growth.

Zappos' experience should not be seen as a critique of holacracy or self-management; the theory behind these structures is solid, but on this occasion, the downfall was in the execution. The system's complexity made it difficult for employees to grasp, ultimately weakening management's influence rather than strengthening it.

Autonomy needs boundaries

So far in this chapter, we have seen different applications of how various executive teams have embraced the principle of distributed autonomy—some with great success, and others, like Zappos, which fell short of success. For any of these structures to facilitate executive influence over the long run, a core psychological criterion needs to be met. And that is the principle of *classification*.

The way our ancestors organised their social structures in prehistoric times continues to shape how humans are wired today.

In early tribes, basic needs like shelter and food were more efficiently met by working together, with each individual contributing their strengths to benefit the whole group. These social dynamics have been ingrained in our behaviour over time, explaining many of our natural tendencies. Evolutionary psychology provides a lens through which we can understand how to design modern organisations for influence by tapping into these instinctive human behaviours, much like how a well-tuned ecosystem thrives when every part works in harmony with its surroundings.

'Classification before calculus' is a fundamental lesson we can take from our physiological roots that should be applied to organisational design. According to evolutionary psychologists, due to the human quest for survival in the Stone Age, we have in our genetic blueprint innate capabilities for sorting and classifying information so we can systematise and simplify a complex world.[10] Classification provided a way to clearly sort members of the tribe, enabling responsibilities and roles to be readily allocated and defined. Our Stone Age ancestors found simplicity in the classification system; every time there was food to share, there was no ambiguity as to who was entitled to what amount of food — the classification system provided a clear, objective answer immediately. This enabled rapid decision-making, which was favoured over doing *calculus* — that is, spending time strategising, analysing, debating, and sometimes, over-engineering.

The idea of classification before calculus can be applied to organisational design to ensure structures remain simple and clear, with well-defined roles and team responsibilities that are aligned. This is critical to success when autonomy is distributed. For external observers, key warning signs when assessing an organisation's design include organisation charts that show unclear or overlapping responsibilities among functional teams.

Frequent reorganisations are another red flag, often indicating an overly complex, 'calculus-heavy' management approach. This constant rethinking of team and functional structures forces employees to repeatedly adapt to new ways of working, hindering the development of a stable and clear system. This gives rise to poor decision-making where autonomy is distributed—who makes the call, and on what kind of decisions?

Evolutionary psychologists counsel that our innate tendency to quickly classify people, situations, and experiences, rather than engaging in nuanced analysis, creates a challenge for management teams. If an organisation's design does not clearly and effectively classify and label functions in straightforward, almost stereotypical ways, management faces an uphill battle against this deeply ingrained human behaviour.[10] Sometimes, the most obvious solution is the best one. In trying to innovate or add more headcount, we often over-engineer, overlooking the simple, common-sense approaches when it comes to people organisation. When roles and responsibilities are easy to understand, people naturally perform better, and teams can focus on delivering results rather than navigating complexity. Simplicity, in many cases, is the key.

One example that came across my desk was an Australian technology company that had undergone a significant restructure as part of its growth and maturation. After the restructure, the business had three executive portfolios that appeared to have significant overlap:

- Executive of Customer Success

- Executive of New Business and Change

- Executive of Technology Design.

There were multiple issues with this structure. First, the labels were not clear. Was the remit of the Customer Success function for existing customers only, given the explicit carve-out of the New Business and Change team? Was New Business only for new customers? What was the 'Change' component? The second issue lay with the Technology Design function, which, in order to deliver effectively, meant it was heavily dependent on first understanding what the customer needed. However, because this function was explicitly quarantined to stand alone, this portfolio's work was completed in isolation without direct feedback from customers—it relied only on the second-hand feedback passed on by the other two teams. I could see that the structure was unclear and would create a siloed approach which, in the context of classification, hampered the executive management team's ability to set clear boundaries for autonomy.

The key question for outsiders to consider is whether the classification of business units aligns with the company's operations. Seek out clearly defined corporate divisions in investor reports. This clarity not only delineates accountability but also establishes structured channels for communication and decision-making. This enables management to effectively convey strategic priorities, provide feedback, and address concerns, ensuring that vital information reaches employees promptly, fostering transparency and alignment with company goals. Moreover, streamlined communication allows management and teams to collaborate efficiently, responding swiftly to emerging issues that could affect project timelines or budgets. In this way, management can meaningfully distribute its autonomy and exert influence internally.

CHAPTER 7

External influence: Attracting a radical base

In this chapter, I introduce the second half of the Influence Scorecard: external influence. This measures an executive team's ability to cultivate a strong and lasting following outside the organisation. Returning to the power grid analogy from Chapter 6, the ideal company is one that attracts crowds of customers waiting eagerly outside, ready to purchase the company's next product. The goal is not just to create a temporary spike in demand, but to foster a loyal, repeat audience that remains engaged long after trends have passed.

For example, consider companies like Apple, which has mastered this art. Customers rarely buy a single product—they become part of a community, eagerly anticipating each new release. This level of external influence ensures long-term loyalty and sustained growth, transcending short-term market fads. It takes years to create a radical base—the types of loyal customers that are convinced whatever the company is selling is unique and desirable.

Think of management teams that have generated immense growth over long periods of time. Nike is another example, given it sells one of the most commoditised and simple products on the market: shoes and sportswear. Even in a heavily competitive market and being founded almost two decades after its key competitors, Adidas and Puma, Nike has been able to overtake its European counterparts to become the largest sportswear company in the world. What the executive management team has achieved better than any other company in this field is rewiring the consumer mindset behind sportswear. No longer were sports shoes seen as a niche piece of equipment. Rather, Nike positioned its sports shoes as performance-enhancing for the everyday sportsperson.

The process that Nike's management undertook to get to such an influential position has been written about by its founder Phil Knight in his book *Shoe Dog*. At first it borrowed the influence from its sponsored athletes. Then it attached itself to the fitness movement by creating running communities and supporting the grassroots street basketball culture. Finally, when it had established itself in the minds of consumers, it went further than most companies by openly taking a stance on political issues. In 2018, at the height of the Black Lives Matter movement, Nike launched a series of marketing campaigns in support of Colin Kaepernick and the social injustice experienced by African Americans. The decision by Nike's executives to join the movement was highly unorthodox. Many thought it would hurt sales and alienate some customers, wondering if it was a risk to take a stance on social issues totally unrelated to Nike's business. The decision to do so certainly went against the typical corporate textbook. But the decision proved brilliant. It solidified Nike's reputation among its loyal followers and target market. Those that were not in Nike's target market were unashamedly (and deliberately) turned away.

Not only was the move to support Kaepernick a brand-building success, financially it drove a 31 per cent increase in sales during the long weekend the campaign was launched. What Nike beautifully illustrates for us is that the path to external influence—that is, influencing customer behaviour—is twofold. A business must first have a unique proposition, and then it must harness that to create a brand that lives and breathes its values, which resonate and align with those of its customers. Building more than a brand—creating a movement.

Top executive management teams have a knack for attracting a passionate following. While not everyone goes all-in on flashy marketing like Nike, they always craft a unique proposition that resonates deeply with their target audience. Curiosity draws people in, and as they experience repeated satisfaction, they evolve from customers to supporters, eventually becoming fervent ambassadors. The relationship shifts from a mere transaction to a rich emotional connection. The ultimate goal? Creating a devoted base of fans who not only prioritise your product but also enthusiastically recruit others.

Achieving this goes beyond just clever branding and marketing. Building a radical base requires executives to infuse every aspect of their vision into the organisation, supported by the right internal set up as discussed in Chapter 6. The standout teams are those that do not just compete on price; they leverage their stellar reputation. Take Costco, for example. Customers are willing to pay for an annual membership based on the belief that Costco offers competitive prices and a vast selection. Does it *always* have the cheapest products? Probably not. But the reputation alone is enough to keep customers loyal and engaged.

In this chapter, we will see how great executive teams build a radical base, how they expand their appeal, and the tell-tale signs of brands that are growing more influential with time.

Uniqueness

In an increasingly competitive environment where customers have more access and more choice, it becomes even more critical to create a unique proposition that elevates a company from its competitors. The largest companies in the world have this—Apple positions itself as luxury tech; Tesla sets itself apart as the automobile newcomer with all the cutting-edge features; Amazon is known for its speedy delivery. But most executive teams do not have the luxury of being the market giant. Instead, they need to find ways to be renowned. But renowned for what?

Do they pursue the path of being renowned for being *better* than the competition? Or do they want to *avoid* the competition? Or maybe they want to be *unique* to the competition?

Striving to be merely better than the competition often leads to the path of greatest resistance. It involves following established practices and attempting to surpass rivals in a head-to-head contest where the incumbent holds the upper hand—unless, of course, you are the incumbent. A clear example of this is the wave of ridesharing apps that emerged after Uber's launch. Globally, consumers now have a multitude of options, including Uber, Sidecar, Lyft, Didi, Ola, and many others, all offering similar propositions and vying to outdo one another. In such scenarios, and often when the strategy focuses solely on 'being better', businesses can fall into the trap of competing primarily on price—a strategy that is neither sustainable nor innovative.

Avoiding the competition is the *blue ocean strategy*[1]—finding new pockets of growth without competition—a viable option for most companies that have not yet been held back by deeply entrenched business models. This is a powerful strategy that has seen many businesses succeed. Revolut is a fantastic example of avoidance strategy. Launched in 2015, the company has a global mission to change the way people bank—avoiding the traditional banking model of physical branches, bureaucracy, and paperwork, and enabling its customers to spend, save, invest, and borrow money (and more) 'in just a few taps' via its mobile app.[2]

Being unique is something else entirely. It is the blue ocean strategy but more. It is about changing—rather, *creating*—the value proposition. The classic example is Netflix, which overhauled the traditional video rental model and replaced it with streaming. Or Apple, when it created the iPad. I recall many years ago receiving the first iPad as a birthday gift from my wife, and my immediate reaction was, 'What do I need this for? I'm not going to use it.' And yet it has become, for me and many others, both a leisure and productivity device that I touch every single day. Apple created for me a need I never knew I had.

Similarly, The Trade Desk is upending the advertising world—it has created a digital platform for advertisers to buy advertising space from those that want to sell advertising space. It has benefited from the digitalisation of advertising and the shift from analogue TV to digital-connected TV. Same again when Microsoft shifted its Microsoft Office suite from a one-off licence to an ongoing software-as-a-service offering.

These are examples of how executive teams have shifted their value proposition and become unique. The same approach can (and should) be applied to the entire persona of a company—the conglomeration of how it presents itself to the world, what it sells, and how it conducts its business. Being unique, in every sense, is core to attracting a radical base. And there is a very simple question to ask (which can be answered through observation, and, measures whether uniqueness has been achieved): How easy is it for competitors to replicate the offering of the business?

High-effort differentiators

There are varying ways companies can differentiate themselves from the competition. Some methods take more effort but deliver a long-lasting positive benefit, whereas others offer quick wins at minimal effort, as shown in figure 7-1.

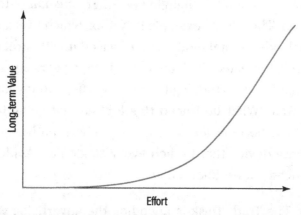

Figure 7-1: Higher effort differentiation initiatives produce outsized long-term value.

Long-term success comes from those management teams willing to persist with the higher effort methods. They require more investment and time, but they also yield outsized benefit. Take, for example, Garmin, named after its co-founders Gary Burrell and Min Kao who started the company in 1989 (more than three decades later, Min Kao still remains as Executive Chairman). It is best known for its smartwatches and GPS devices in a hyper-competitive industry that has seen many competitors come and go. Garmin's management team demonstrates how a company, in the face of heavy competition, can still stand out and find its own radical base of customers. It has done this by persisting and iterating its products to differentiate its brand and appeal to a unique target market.

The process to find its niche was not smooth. Rather, it was a series of iterations that remains an ongoing process today. In its initial phase, Garmin supplied the US military with GPS systems and experienced enormous growth when it took that technology to the mass market through its GPS watches, marine navigation devices, and personal GPS trackers. During this period, it created a diversified range of GPS products and leveraged its first-mover advantage to edge ahead of TomTom, its main rival in that era. But by the mid-2000s, smartphones started to emerge, and their embedded GPS functionality began eroding the market for Garmin's personal GPS devices. Executives knew the company had to stand out again. Big investments were made in developing its own smartphone via a partnership with ASUS but it failed—it was simply an inferior version of Apple and Samsung smartphones. Then it attempted its own navigation app, which also struggled against Google Maps and its more up-to-date street information. Playing follow-the-leader was not going to work. Instead, Garmin needed to define its own path.

The management team went back to the drawing board, leveraging its wide product range as a core advantage. It had a foothold in many segments, including automotive, marine, and aviation, but the fastest growth rates were seen in wearables.[3] So while the automotive GPS market was under attack from the rise of smartphones, Garmin made wearables the next horizon of growth, investing heavily in developing its smart watches for fitness and outdoor applications. It worked. Building on its radical base of outdoorsy types, it offered product differentiation because its watches focused on accurate and detailed location measurements, altitude and longer battery life—all things that other smart watches lacked. Fitbit was focused on the lower end of the market. Apple and Samsung were focused on integrating music, phone calls, and other mobile phone applications into their watches.

And by gearing its products towards specific outdoors and fitness use cases, Garmin was able to stand out again.

Executive management teams that increase product development frequency iterate faster and are more likely to unlock new product differentiators. Garmin did this successfully as it discovered its winning formula with wearables. It tailored its products for specific target market segments, allowing it to build a reputation in elite fitness wearables. From there, it has expanded its product range to capture a wider audience.

Competing through product differentiation demands considerable effort. It requires persistence with substantial research and development to stay aligned with the latest technologies, and the need for frequent updates makes it an expensive strategy for newcomers to imitate. However, the investment paid off in Garmin's case, as it created significant barriers for competitors, allowing the company to further solidify its position in its niche markets.

Another company that has harnessed the power of high effort differentiators is Dino Polska, a grocery chain in Poland that has grown from a market cap of US$1 billion in 2017 into US$10 billion in 2024. During that time, store numbers have expanded from 775 to over 2000. The management team, led by founder Tomasz Biernacki, has proven that even in the most commoditised markets, it is possible to stand out from the crowd and attract a radical base. Unlike Garmin, which relied on product and target market differentiation, there is no single product; rather, its grocery stores are stockists for other brands. But the executive management team at Dino Polska has taken a different angle—it has differentiated itself via its store network and shop format. Each store is standardised and roughly 400 square metres in size—much smaller than warehouse-like supermarkets, but larger than the average convenience store. Due to each store's nimble setup, the company can locate itself closer to its customers, targeting those who live on the outskirts of population-dense areas. This format and network is unique, offering the access of a convenience store with the breadth of stock of a supermarket (each store stocks around 5000 products). Shoppers find this format convenient as they can drive and park close to the shop. The model has proven successful with customers, allowing Dino Polska to rinse and repeat the same store setup across the country.

To compete effectively with other grocery stores, pricing still matters, even though it is not a primary point of differentiation for Dino Polska's executive team. On that front, it ensures prices are kept low by reducing overheads. For example, the company sources, warehouses and distributes its own meat, owns the land each store sits on (avoiding rental costs), and has solar panels installed on over 80 per cent of its stores (reducing electricity costs). Figure 7-2 shows Dino Polska's net profit since its IPO listing.

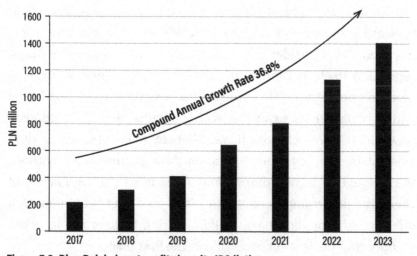

Figure 7-2: Dino Polska's net profit since its IPO listing.

There are numerous ways executive teams can differentiate their companies. Garmin has chosen to differentiate its products and target niche markets. Dino Polska has built a distribution network that requires significant investment in store rollout and adopted a unique shop format that is difficult to replicate—it would require competitors to renovate their shopfronts. In the long run, methods that require more effort deliver exponential benefit. The point of difference, if executed well, allows a company to distance itself from the crowd and therefore compete in another dimension. It can then become known for its uniqueness, which is the first step to attracting a radical base.

Even in industries where everything seems commoditised, there is always room to stand out and be unique. Great executive teams can still differentiate themselves by elevating the customer experience to new heights. This is relatively straightforward for outsiders to see—engage directly with the company, and you can witness and assess this distinctive experience for yourself.

The customer promise

The ability to expand into new markets and regions while preserving the strengths that have made a business successful is a refined skill. Consider how a traditional car manufacturer might reposition itself in the electric vehicle market amid a surge of modern competitors. How does it harness its established brand and manufacturing expertise without being seen as outdated? New electric vehicle companies benefit from starting with a clean slate, shaping their reputation through innovation without the baggage of legacy perceptions. This is where the finesse of executive leadership comes into play—evolving the company's offerings and public image while ensuring it does not lose the identity that made it recognisable in the first place.

In the case where a company seeks to expand overseas, the reputation it holds in its home country may not carry the same prestige in the new country—or it may even be perceived negatively. As I write, Meituan, China's leading food delivery company, has announced plans to expand into new countries. In China, it has built a reputation for being a fast delivery platform that is backed by a large cohort of deliverers. The promotions it offers to customers encourages them to order from the Meituan platform, increasing the number of jobs available for deliverers so they can earn more. On the other side, it can offer preferential rates for deliverers who improve the network delivery times for customers—this virtuous cycle creates a platform that reinforces its advantage over time. But when it comes to overseas expansions, this advantage does not translate. Meituan needs to start from scratch and compete with incumbent food delivery platforms that are already entrenched with customers.

Meituan has embraced a multi-brand strategy, deploying distinct sub-brands tailored to each geographical market it enters. This approach has been evident in its expansion into Hong Kong. As for its venture into the Middle East, the future remains uncertain and the outcomes yet to unfold. However, one thing is clear: For Meituan to succeed in its expansion, it must uphold the same high standards of service for its customers, vendors, and delivery partners that it has maintained in China, despite the varied cultural expectations in its new markets.

Another example of a company that has continued building a reliable and trusted business even though it has evolved its business over the course of two decades started out as an eBay copy-cat before morphing into an ecommerce giant. It is a business that stretches across retail, logistics, payment systems, and financial services. That company is MercadoLibre, a US$80 billion market cap company founded in 1999 by Marcos Galperin—he still owns 7 per cent of the company 25 years later. The name MercadoLibre is Spanish for 'free market'. It is befitting for such a company given it started life as a technology firm in Argentina but has expanded across South America with its mission of 'democratising commerce'.

In the beginning, as a platform business that relied on connecting buyers and sellers, it was essential to build trust. Without a strong reputation for trust, shoppers would be reluctant to enter their credit card details; merchants would not open an account and list their products. Keep in mind that in the early 2000s, the buying and selling of goods online was not common—South America had low internet usage rates, low appetite for credit cards, and unreliable delivery logistics infrastructure, which meant MercadoLibre had significant work to do to change the mindset of the population. The challenge was enormous. Many US-based ecommerce giants contemplating an expansion put South America in the too-hard basket, preferring the low-hanging fruit of US and European customers.[4] However, the region had a large population and so MercadoLibre's executive team, which consisted of South Americans, saw these challenges more as an opportunity than a barrier. The key to growing the business would boil down to the promise of trust. And that has been the philosophy from the very first day.

Since the early 2000s, the promise has remained the same, which maintains trust from MercadoLibre's customers. It is the key to how MercadoLibre has built its radical base, enabling it to possess a ready group of willing customers every time it launches a new product, thus adding to its value proposition. Small to medium sized enterprises comprise 67 per cent of its merchant base—a cohort that has been individually won over with the same promise:

Trust us to manage your transaction. Take for instance when MercadoLibre moved into payments in 2003. Back then, online transactions were rare given the low usage of credit cards in South America. So MercadoLibre had to set up an escrow system with a physical network of agents that would receive cash from buyers, triggering merchants to release their goods and receive their cash payment. It was a clunky solution compared to today's electronic approach. However, the uptake was high. Within three years the expansion into payments represented 8 per cent of its transaction value.

It was much the same when MercadoLibre opened its logistics service in 2013. Its radical base was already warm to the idea of handing over delivery responsibilities to the company. They trusted its offering and were happy to switch over from national mailing services.

Although MercadoLibre's suite of services has evolved with the times, its promise and identity never has, enabling it to continue building upon the trust it has engendered with customers. And that is how its executive management team has balanced the fine art of evolution and adaptation. It is symbolic that the company's simplistic and unsophisticated logo has remained the same since 2000—a simple image showing a handshake between two people, enclosed in an oval icon. Even the blue and yellow theme has remained much the same. The illustrated handshake is almost identical from a quarter of a century ago, symbolic of the promise of trust MercadoLibre made to its users all those years ago. This familiarity is what its radical base has come to expect.

Circling back to the example of Meituan—whichever path it decides to take to achieve geographical expansion, its path to success will rely on its already established reputation in China. It is known for convenience to orderers, hotels, restaurants, and deliverers. Even though the global expansion poses a different set of challenges, Meituan's solution for each market can be different — but its customer promise needs to remain the same if it wants to continue building its radical base.

Building a movement

When executive teams align their brands with broader societal values, they transcend mere product sales and tap into larger cultural currents. Nike exemplified this by embracing sports culture when expanding into China, and now Lululemon is doing the same with the surge in yoga and wellness. These companies are not simply saying, 'buy our products'; they are inviting their customers to join a lifestyle and community centred around health and wellness, proudly positioning themselves as leading advocates of these values.

You can spot when a brand is transforming into a movement because their behaviour stops being about them and starts being about what they represent. The signs are everywhere, from their advertising to who is wearing their gear. Take a stroll through certain neighbourhoods and you will see Lululemon everywhere on the backs of health-conscious, yoga-loving types.

When a movement catches on, it is like a powerful wave that lifts the brands who have nailed their positioning. So, what are some of the signs that a company is cleverly building a movement?

Keeping it real

Look for companies that are unapologetically themselves. Just like with individuals, true authenticity draws people in and creates a loyal following. Yet, for many corporations, this is a tough feat due to structural constraints. Short-term investor demands and the fear of standing out can make sticking to a unique path seem risky. Executives often focus on immediate results during their limited tenure, favouring existing brand personas and quick campaigns over the long-term build of a radical customer base.

In contrast, founder-led companies or those with long-tenured CEOs are often set up for long-term brand success. With less pressure to deliver short-term gains, these companies can focus on shaping a distinct identity. Great executive teams understand that they are free to craft a brand personality that resonates deeply with their customers. This involves a cohesive approach where every aspect of the company—product development, pricing, distribution, branding, and marketing—aligns with the core values and personality of the brand. Take Rolex, for example. Its prestige is built on a careful balance of all these elements, managed in harmony. It is not just about marketing or product development alone; it is about having the freedom to pursue a unique path and cultivate a devoted following over time.

This is what Patagonia discovered. Yvon Chouinard officially founded the business in 1973, but he already had a predecessor company called Chouinard Equipment that was known for its specialist rock climbing equipment. The tale of how Chouinard Equipment started not only explains why Patagonia is one of the world's most successful privately owned brands today, but also how being genuine and consistent with a brand philosophy will attract a radical base.

Chouinard shares the story of when he started rock climbing in the 1960s.[5] Back then, rock climbers wanted to assert human dominance over a mountain. Just like planting a flag on the moon, rock climbers wanted to leave their pegs in the rocks as a proud sign of their successful climb, but also to help others who would follow in their path. Chouinard never shared the same mindset of domination. He wanted to leave the mountain in its original state so others could conquer it as nature had designed, untarnished by the marks of humans prior. This in itself is illustrative of one of the foundational values that Patagonia began with and is known for still—'environmentalism: protect our home planet'.[6] This was only possible with higher-quality pegs than what were available at the time, which prompted him to learn basic blacksmithing techniques and create his own equipment. Higher-quality pegs were required because they needed to be removed, reused, and relied upon repeatedly for a single climb. These pegs were designed to be sturdy permanent equipment that would follow the climber back down the mountain. Gradually, he started selling these pegs to friends and so Chouinard Equipment was born.

The desire to enjoy nature in its purest form is what inspired the founding of Patagonia, and for over five decades, the company has remained unwavering in that mission. Every initiative Patagonia has launched aligns with this original philosophy, rooted in its core values of environmental protection and sustainable product development. Worn Wear, a subsidiary, focuses on repairing and recycling outdoor gear and clothing, while Patagonia Provisions offers sustainable food products. Long before sustainability became a widespread concern, Patagonia pioneered its own rigorous sustainability standards.

Led by Yvon Chouinard, the executive team at Patagonia has been developing a genuine values-backed brand personality, which has been reinforced over decades of consistent action. Genuineness is key. Its radical base was small at the beginning, rock climbers primarily, but over time it has ended up, ironically, in Wall Street and Silicon Valley, where many young 'tech bros' and 'finance bros' see Patagonia vests as a symbol of an iconoclastic take on the traditional suit and tie—signalling 'I may be a banker but I hike and I'm environmentally conscious.'

In 2022, Yvon Chouinard transferred his entire ownership of Patagonia to two entities:

- The Patagonia Purpose Trust (a holding company that will retain 100 per cent voting control and act as the moral and philosophical compass)

- The Holdfast Collective (which will donate 100 per cent of Patagonia's profits to fight the climate crisis).

With the transfer of ownership, Patagonia will remain privately held forever (as Chouinard has envisioned) and its profits will go towards saving the planet.

Management teams are often tempted to change their persona depending on the flavour of the decade, or to refresh the market's view of the business. Watch out for the corporate rebrand. It may be climate change this decade, but last decade it was embracing technology. This is a mistake. Influence is lost every time there is a change in company persona—the radical base that may have been forming can only crystallise over many decades of implementation of a consistent and genuine philosophy. Patience is key here. Patagonia and Rolex have shown how this can be done successfully. As Yvon Chouinard says: 'Brands move people, not goods.' And that is what great executive teams understand.

Grabbing the conch

One of the most observable tests for any executive team is its ability to rally a dedicated following of loyal customers. True leaders are not shy about seizing this opportunity with both hands.

Often, social media—a powerful tool for personal engagement and influence—is either underestimated or handed off to internal PR teams. Yet, when used creatively, social media can forge deep, personal connections with customers, transforming their perceptions and interactions with the brand. It is not just about publicity; it is about building genuine relationships and harnessing the collective power of your audience.

Consider the way Elon Musk uses social media. His heavy involvement in running Tesla, X, and SpaceX would be reason enough to forgo his social media account and interviews with podcasters and journalists. Despite his busy schedule, he makes time for media engagement. There is a commercial reason—it allows him to build a personal media presence, which he then leverages to promote his companies and his product launches. The controversy he creates with publicity stunts captures the attention of his supporters, while deliberately alienating others that are unlikely to be customers. As his companies are all future-focused, he stands to benefit from asserting his views on new technologies and playing up his brash, anti-establishment persona as many of his followers share the same mentality. His companies are disruptive; his followers are early adopters of technology. In addition, he has built up a cult following by creating a movement much greater than himself or his company. Tesla represents human advancement towards electric vehicles and environmental sustainability—all themes that resonate with the direction society has been heading towards. By elevating the brand's association with a movement, the influence Elon Musk and his executive team have over Tesla's radical base is magnified.

But the use of technology and social media is not the only way to grow a following. There are many who use much older methods just as effectively. Warren Buffett has made only a handful of social media posts but over decades has created a cult of followers and fellow investors. His annual general meetings for Berkshire Hathaway have attracted investors worldwide, dubbed by Warren Buffett as 'Woodstock for capitalists'. His movement is value investing—a style that favours buying undervalued companies and holding them for long periods of time. By positioning Berkshire Hathaway as the pre-eminent value investing firm, Warren Buffett is able to elevate beyond self-promotion and become the spiritual leader of an investment movement. Through his annual letters, Warren Buffett has espoused conventional wisdom to create his own common-sense approach to financial markets—a style that has attracted a wide following of self-driven investors.

What stands out with executives that can successfully influence their radical base is the sincerity and genuineness. Whether they are brash like Elon Musk, or self-deprecating like Warren Buffett, they are unafraid to reveal their true feelings. They are not fence-sitters. They are unafraid to stand for something and willing to polarise if it means being true to their values. They have embraced their own style and take a confident approach, which is attractive to their radical base. So long as the media exposure is related to and aligned with the company's mission, outsiders should see this as a positive signal that executives know how to leverage their media presence.

PART III: RECAP

How influential is management?

♦ Outsiders should focus on the fundamental principles of management's ability to influence:

Influence Scorecard

INTERNAL		EXTERNAL	
Proximity to Customers	/ 10	Uniqueness	/ 10
Distributed Autonomy	/ 10	Building a Movement	/ 10
Total Score	/ 40		

♦ The typical corporate pyramid impedes a company as it grows.

♦ Management's ability to influence its internal teams is only possible if it has the right setup. Look for companies with minimal hierarchical layers. Five or less is ideal; eight or nine is excessive.

♦ Information needs to flow freely. Look for objective measures — are there formal policies and practices? Insider knowledge helps, otherwise ask questions at Annual General Meetings.

♦ Think small to grow big — look for organisational structures that limit the size of their divisions (and are aware of Dunbar's number of 150 people).

♦ Decentralised structures harness entrepreneurialism, counteract social loafing, and increase management's influence with employees.

♦ Look for conglomerates that split their group up into smaller companies/divisions...

- ... But this only works if roles are clear with boundaries; check that executive titles make logical sense, and business units align with the business's operations.

- Competing head-on if you are the challenger is fraught with risk. Favour companies that elevate themselves beyond the competition in high-effort areas.

- High effort = difficult/costly/takes a long time for competitors to replicate.

- Companies with fast product development cycles will hasten the discovery of what customers truly want, even if they fail initially.

- Companies that rebrand and change their customer promise lose momentum.

- Management teams can evolve their offering, but they must keep the same promise to their customers or risk losing what they have built.

- Look for companies that stand for something, unafraid in their pursuit of a particular demographic, even if means alienating others.

- Influencing customers is a long game — identify companies that are prepared to make genuine and consistent customer promises over long periods of time, and stay the course.

- Keep your eyes peeled for companies that transcend their own brand. They no longer advertise for themselves; they advocate for a movement.

- Look for executives that are unafraid to use the media to their advantage, creating a movement that transcends their company. The movement should be in line with where society is headed.

Epilogue: If you know, you know

Open on my computer, as I write this book, is a small ribbon of blue and purple sitting in the bottom right-hand corner of my monitor. It is an application icon that forced itself there a few months ago without my permission. Now it sits next to the time and date on my dock, like a friendly neighbour that has just moved in without warning, waving at me. Microsoft calls it Copilot, its latest artificial intelligence (AI) tool. Its presence is symbolic of the era in which we live—one of rapid advancement. Yesterday it was augmented reality and the metaverse; tomorrow it will be robotics and biotechnology. Now every management report I read, every management team I meet, mentions generative AI as though it will be a game changer for their business. But I know these are just tools. Sure, we are witnessing a wave of new tools, but how companies harness those tools is down to the skill of the management team. Companies grow because of people. People come up with strategies, execute them, and get rewarded if they are successful. People drive growth, not tools.

Next to the ribbon is my calendar. I click on it and am reminded of a company I am due to visit in Japan in a few weeks. I am looking forward to meeting its management team. It has all the hallmarks I look for—a founder-led company that has shown excellent judgement over the past 10 years and is now increasingly active in influencing its customer base of small-to-medium enterprises. No doubt it will be impacted by AI given it is a software company. Is the management team adopting AI? How far progressed is it?

No, those are not the right questions, they are much too superficial. They do not drive at the heart of value creation. I am more interested in how the executive management team makes decisions, its mindset, who is involved, and what the dynamics are. Does the team have the capacity to make bold decisions for the long term?

Next come the questions about its alignment with shareholders. Being founder-led, I can already assume a base level of cohesion. But what about the rest of the executive team? How is each executive's performance measured and how are they incentivised? Are they spending time and resources on growing the brand? The answers to these questions give me insight into the people behind the company.

Next come the company's ability to win over employees and customers. It has just embarked on an aggressive TV advertising strategy—is it a unique proposition for customers? How is the organisation set up and how does it deploy talent for each of the products it offers?

Those are the real topics of interest. With time, everything else will fall into place (including all things related to AI) if its judgement, alignment, and influence is exceptional.

This Japanese company is one of many—I have only scratched the surface. Most of the companies I have mentioned in this book are founder-led. And like many that I have researched and have interested me, they all have a unique take on management philosophy. In this wonderful species (which I estimate to be around 2000–3000 listed globally), you will find a propensity to do things differently to the conventional corporate textbook. These companies have more freedom to operate independently and have a longer-term horizon than most other companies. They also have the structures in place that help them avoid the group cognitive biases prevalent in large bureaucratic organisations.

I open a browser to read the news—more AI. This time its Jensen Huang, founder of NVIDIA, who is the keynote speaker at a conference themed on the future of computing. The headline reads 'The future is generative' and the journalist focuses on the most provocative highlights from his speech which, amid the current euphoria for AI, makes it read like the next gold rush is about to kick off.

Influence. Any prediction about the future seems to involve some discussion about Jensen Huang and NVIDIA. NVIDIA equals the future—not a bad way to associate with a movement, right?

I reflect on my own journey. There is a rush when you find special companies run by brilliant executives—the process of seeking them out, assessing their management teams, studying them, filtering them, learning from them, and understanding their long game. There are so many management teams hard at work, all with varying styles and philosophies on how to maximise growth. Only the special ones stand out, and while there are many paths to success, they all share a common set of traits to get there.

For these companies, it is not what they have already achieved but their *potential* that is the most exciting. When it comes to assessing management, as they say: If you know, you know. After all, I am a founder myself.

Acknowledgements

First and foremost, to my incredible wife—my greatest supporter, my unwavering cheerleader, and the one who embodies the Founder Framework in the most personal and inspiring way. You've been my constant teammate, and together we lift each other higher every step of the way. I couldn't imagine this journey without you by my side.

A heartfelt thank you to Simon for your mentorship and friendship. Every conversation leaves me energised and more confident in my path.

To Ian and Phil, your introductions have played a pivotal role in shaping the insights within this book.

A special thank you to the team at Wiley—Lucy, Leigh, Ingrid, Kerry and Renee—for your guidance, patience, and steadfast support in embracing my idea and shaping it into a book.

And to you—the reader—thank you for being part of this first chapter of my writing journey. Stay tuned, there's more ahead.

References

Introduction

1. Lam, Lawrence (2023). 'Chemist Warehouse founder
   reveals his success secrets'. *Morningstar*. Available at:
   https://www.morningstar.com.au/insights/stocks/235554/
   chemist-warehouse-founder-reveals-his-success-secrets

2. Perepu, Indu (IBS Center for Management Research) (2016). 'Nike
   in China'. *The Case Centre: Teaching note Reference no. 216-0055-8*.
   Available at: https://www.thecasecentre.org/products/view?id=137226

Part I

1. Abdullah (2023). 'From a small trading company to a tech giant: The
   inspiring story of Samsung's founder'. *Medium*. Available at: https://
   medium.com/@imabd489/from-a-small-trading-company-to-a-tech-
   giant-the-inspiring-story-of-samsungs-founder-904126263c4e

2. Lankov, Andrei (2011). 'Lee Byung-Chull: founder of Samsung
   Group'. *The Korea Times*. Available at: https://www.koreatimes
   .co.kr/www/news/issues/2014/01/363_96557.html

3. Lee, Kun-Hee (2010). 'Business Philosophy of Lee Byung-Chull'. *The Korea Times*. Available at: https://www.koreatimes.co.kr/www/tech/2024/08/129_60674.html

4. Kaur, Komalpreet, Zhao, Elena and Trifan, Vanina Adoriana (2023). 'A story of vision and leadership: Unveiling the Samsung Electronics brand's path to success'. *'Ovidius' University Annals, Economic Sciences Series*, Volume 23(2), pp. 491–500. Available at: https://stec.univ-ovidius.ro/html/anale/ENG/wp-content/uploads/2024/02/13-2.pdf

5. Kim, Miyoung (2020). 'Samsung's Lee: Tainted titan who built a global tech giant'. *Reuters*. Available at: https://www.reuters.com/article/idUSKBN27A019/

6. Cain, Geoffrey (2020). *Samsung Rising: The Inside Story of the South Korean Giant That Set Out to Beat Apple and Conquer Tech*. Currency.

Chapter 1

1. Robison, Peter (2021). *Flying Blind: The 737 MAX tragedy and the fall of Boeing*. Doubleday.

2. Klee, Miles (2024). 'A complete timeline of the Boeing 737 MAX disaster'. *Rolling Stone*. Available at: https://www.rollingstone.com/culture/culture-features/boeing-737-max-disasters-timeline-1235007089/

3. Reuters (2024). 'Boeing's ongoing 737 MAX crisis'. *Reuters*. Available at: https://www.reuters.com/business/aerospace-defense/boeings-ongoing-737-max-crisis-2024-01-06/

4. Löscher, Peter (2012). 'The CEO of Siemens on using a scandal to drive change'. *Harvard Business Review*. Available at: https://hbr.org/2012/11/the-ceo-of-siemens-on-using-a-scandal-to-drive-change

5. Schubert, Siri and Miller, T. Christian (2008). 'At Siemens, bribery was just a line item'. *The New York Times*. Available at: https://www.nytimes.com/2008/12/21/business/worldbusiness/21siemens.html

6. Dietz, Graham and Gillespie, Nicole (2012). 'Rebuilding trust: How Siemens atoned for its sins'. *The Guardian*. Available at: https://www.theguardian.com/sustainable-business/recovering-business-trust-siemens

7. Alonso, Tefi (2022). 'How Siemens became a multinational technology conglomerate'. *Cascade*. Available at: https://www.cascade.app/studies/siemens-strategy-study

8. Fung, Brian and Tsukayama, Hayley (2016). 'Behind Yahoo's downfall: Bad bets and failure to adapt'. *The Chicago Tribune*. Available at: https://www.chicagotribune.com/2016/04/20/behind-yahoos-downfall-bad-bets-and-failure-to-adapt/

9. Vara, Vauhina (2016). 'Why Yahoo couldn't adapt to the smartphone era'. *The New Yorker*. Available at: https://www.newyorker.com/business/currency/why-yahoo-couldnt-adapt-to-the-iphone-era

10. *S&P Capital IQ* (with Lumenary Investment Management analysis).

Chapter 2

1. Insurance Journal (2009). 'Exclusive video interview with William R. Berkley, take 2: Diversity and decentralization'. *Insurance Journal*. Available at: https://www.youtube.com/watch?v=0b-n43VMUgw

2. Verbanas, Patti (2012). 'Pay it forward'. *Leader's Edge*. Available at: https://www.leadersedge.com/lifestyle/pay-it-forward

3. Lam, Lawrence (2024). 'Graham Turner on lessons from 40+ years of Flight Centre'. *Firstlinks*. Available at: https://www.firstlinks .com.au/graham-turner-lessons-40-plus-years-flight-centre-pt1

4. Lam, Lawrence (2024). 'Graham Turner on lessons from 40+ years of Flight Centre, Part 2'. *Firstlinks*. Available at: https://www.firstlinks.com.au/ graham-turner-lessons-learned-40-plus-years-flight-centre-pt2

5. W. R. Berkley (2024). '2023 Annual Report'. *W.R.* Berkley. Available at: https://ir.berkley.com/financials/annual-reports/ default.aspx

6. Chamberlain, Andrew (2012). 'Why do employees stay? A clear career path and good pay, for starters'. *Harvard Business Review*. Available at: https://hbr.org/2017/03/why-do-employees-stay-a-clear-career-path-and-good-pay-for-starters

7. Tufvesson, Angela (2021). 'Staying put'. *LSJ Online*. Available at: https://lsj.com.au/articles/staying-put/

8. Nalbantian, Dana (2024). 'What young associates want from modern law firms'. *Work Design Magazine*. Available at: https://www.workdesign.com/2024/02/what-young-associates-want-from-modern-law-firms/

9. Gagliardi, Nicole (2023). 'Workers' tenure and firm productivity: New evidence from matches employer-employee panel data'. *Industrial Relations* 62(1): pp. 3–33. Available at: https:// onlinelibrary.wiley.com/doi/10.1111/irel.12309

10. Chondrogiannos, Thodoris (2020). 'How a global call centre giant (mis)managed the pandemic'. *Investigate Europe*. Available at: https://www.investigate-europe.eu/posts/how-one-of-the-worlds-biggest-call-centre-companies-mismanaged-the-pandemic-crisis

11. Australian Customer Experience Professionals Association (2023). '2022 Australian contact centres best practice report'. *Australian Customer Experience Professionals Association*. Available at: https://acxpa.com.au/2022-australian-contact-centres-best-practice-report/

Chapter 3

1. Tayan, Brian (2019). 'The Wells Fargo cross-selling scandal'. *Harvard Law School Forum on Corporate Governance*. Available at: https://corpgov.law.harvard.edu/2019/02/06/the-wells-fargo-cross-selling-scandal-2/

2. Kahneman, Daniel and Tversky, Amos (1979). 'Prospect Theory: An analysis of decision under risk'. *Econometrica* 47(2): pp. 263–292. Available at: https://www.jstor.org/stable/1914185

Part II

1. Ryan, Richard M and Deci, Edward L (2000). 'Self-determination theory and the facilitation of intrinsic motivation, social development, and well-being'. *American Psychologist* 55(1): pp. 68–78.

2. Deci, Edward L, Koestner, R and Ryan, Richard M (1999). A meta-analytic review of experiments examining the effects of extrinsic rewards on intrinsic motivation. *Psychological Bulletin* 125(6): pp. 627–668.

3. Pierce, Jon L, Kostova, Tatiana and Dirks, Kurt T (2003). 'The state of psychological ownership: Integrating and extending a century of research'. *Review of General Psychology* 7(1): pp. 84–107.

4. Pierce, Jon L, Kostova, Tatiana and Dirks, Kurt (2001). 'Toward a theory of psychological ownership in organizations'. *Academy of Management Review* 26(2): pp. 298–310.

5. Shurtleff, William and Aoyagi, Akiko (2004). 'K. S. Lo and Vitasoy in Hong Kong and North America: Work with soyfoods'. *Soy Info Center*. Available at: https://www.soyinfocenter.com/HSS/ks_lo_and_vitasoy.php

6. Chamorro-Premuzic, Tomas (2013). 'Does money really affect motivation? A review of the research'. *Harvard Business Review*. Available at: https://hbr.org/2013/04/does-money-really-affect-motiv

7. Morse, Gardiner (2023). 'Why we misread motives'. *Harvard Business Review*. Available at: https://hbr.org/2003/01/why-we-misread-motives

8. Falk, Stefan (2023). 'Understanding the power of motivation'. *Harvard Business Review*. Available at: https://hbr.org/2023/03/understand-the-power-of-intrinsic-motivation

Chapter 4

1. Bebchuk, Lucian A and Fried, Jesse M (2004). 'Pay without performance: The unfulfilled promise of executive compensation'. *Harvard University Press*. Available at: https://ssrn.com/abstract=537783

2. Kilduff, Gavin J (2014). 'Driven to win: Rivalry, motivation, and performance'. *Social Psychological and Personality Science* 5(8): pp. 944–952.

3. Marriott International (2024). '2024 proxy statement'. *Marriott International*. Available at: https://marriott.gcs-web.com/proxy

4. Paycom (2024). '2024 proxy statement'. *Paycom*. Available at: https://investors.paycom.com/financials/sec-filings/

5. Brunello Cucinelli (2024). 'Report on the remuneration policy and compensation paid by Brunello Cucinelli S.P.A. prepared

pursuant to art. 123-TER of the Italian legislative decree no. 58/1998. Approved by the board of directors of the company at the meeting of March 14, 2024'. *Brunello Cucinelli*. Available at: https://investor .brunellocucinelli.com/yep-content/media/Report_on_the_ remuneration_policy_and_compensation_paid:for_the_2023_FY.pdf

6. Brunello Cucinelli (2023). 'Annual financial report — consolidated financial statements as at 31 December 2023'. *Brunello Cucinelli*. Available at: https://investor.brunellocucinelli.com/en/services/ archive/investor/financial-reports/2023

Chapter 5

1. Di Domenico, Stefano I and Ryan, Richard M (2017). 'The merging neuroscience of intrinsic motivation: A new frontier in self-determination research'. *Frontiers in Human Neuroscience* 11: 145.

2. Deci, Edward L and Ryan, Richard M (2013). *Intrinsic Motivation and Self-Determination in Human Behavior.* Springer US.

3. Panksepp, Jaak and Biven, Lucy (2012). *The Archaeology of Mind: Neuroevolutionary origins of human emotions* (Norton Series on Interpersonal Neurobiology). Norton and Company.

4. Pink, Daniel H (2011). *Drive: The surprising truth about what motivates us.* Penguin Putnam Inc.

5. Elliot, AJ (2005). 'A conceptual history of the achievement goal framework.' In Elliot, AJ and Dweck, CS (eds): *Handbook of Competence and Motivation*. Guilford Press, pp. 16–25.

6. Lam, Lawrence (2023). 'Chemist Warehouse founder reveals his success secrets'. *Morningstar*. Available at: https://www .morningstar.com.au/insights/stocks/235554/chemist-warehouse-founder-reveals-his-success-secrets

7. Lam, Lawrence (2023). 'The rise and rise of Chemist Warehouse'. *Morningstar*. Available at: https://www.morningstar.com.au/insights/personal-finance/235983/the-rise-and-rise-of-chemist-warehouse

8. Lam, Lawrence (2022). 'How Barry Lambert beat the banks at their own game'. *Firstlinks*. Available at: https://www.firstlinks.com.au/barry-lambert-beat-banks-game

9. Talevski, Julia (2013). 'Starting up all over again'. *ARN*.

Part III

1. History.com (2017). 'The disastrous backstory behind the invention of LEGO bricks'. *History.com*. Available at: https://www.history.com/news/the-disastrous-backstory-behind-the-invention-of-lego-bricks

2. The LEGO Group (2024). 'The LEGO Group recognised as the most reputable company in the world for the second consecutive year'. *The LEGO Group*. Available at: https://www.lego.com/en-gb/aboutus/news/2024/april/reptrak-2024

3. The LEGO Group (2023). '2023 annual report'. *The LEGO Group*. Available at: https://www.lego.com/cdn/cs/aboutus/assets/blt7e9167f47da173a6/FINAL_Annual_Report_2023.pdf

4. Anderson, Peter and Ross, Jeanne W (2016). 'Transforming the LEGO Group for the digital economy'. *Sloan School of Management*. Available at: https://ctl.mit.edu/sites/ctl.mit.edu/files/attachments/MIT_CISRwp407_TheLEGOGroup_AndersenRoss_0.pdf

5. Rosen, Bob (2014). 'Leadership journeys: LEGO's Jørgen Vig Knudstorp'. *IEDP*. Available at: https://www.iedp.com/articles/leadership-journeys-legos-joergen-vig-knudstorp/

Chapter 6

1. Lam, Lawrence (2024). 'Graham Turner on lessons from 40+ years of Flight Centre'. *Firstlinks*. Available at: https://www.firstlinks.com.au/graham-turner-lessons-40-plus-years-flight-centre-pt1

2. Lam, Lawrence (2024). 'Graham Turner on lessons from 40+ years of Flight Centre, Part 2'. *Firstlinks*. Available at: https://www.firstlinks.com.au/graham-turner-lessons-learned-40-plus-years-flight-centre-pt2

3. Nicholson, Nigel (1997). 'Evolutionary psychology: Toward a new view of human nature and organizational society'. *Human Relations* 50(9): pp. 1053–1078.

4. Johnson, Mandy (2011). *Family Village Tribe*. Penguin Random House.

5. LVMH (2024). 'History'. *LVMH*. Available at: https://www.lvmh.com/our-group/history

6. Thai, Jenny (2016). 'The story behind Zappos's shift to holacracy'. *Wavelength*. Available at: https://wavelength.asana.com/zappos-self-managed-team/

7. Glaeser, Edward (2012). *Triumph of the City*. Penguin Random House.

8. Bernstein, Ethan, Bunch, John, Canner, Niko and Lee, Michael Y (2016). 'Beyond the holacracy hype'. *Harvard Business Review*. Available at: https://hbr.org/2016/07/beyond-the-holacracy-hype

9. Madore, Kevin P and Wagner, Anthony (2019). 'Multicosts of multitasking'. *Cerebrum* 2019:cer-04-19.

10. Nicholson, Nigel (1998). 'How hardwired is human behavior?'. *Harvard Business Review*. Available at: https://hbr.org/1998/07/how-hardwired-is-human-behavior

Chapter 7

1. Kim, W Chan and Mauborgne, Renée (2004). 'Blue ocean strategy'. *Harvard Business Review*. Available at: https://hbr.org/2004/10/blue-ocean-strategy

2. Revolut (2024). 'About us'. *Revolut*. Available at: https://www.revolut.com/en-AU/about/

3. Edwards Jr, Leon (2015). 'Garmin case study'. Slideshare. Available at: https://www.slideshare.net/slideshow/garmin-case-study/55392208

4. Barnett, William, Mekikian, Gary and Johnson, Christy (2020). 'The rise of Mercado Libre'. *Stanford Business School, Case No IB109*. Available at: https://www.gsb.stanford.edu/faculty-research/case-studies/rise-mercado-libre

5. Miller, Mark and Conley, Lucas (2018). *Legacy in the Making: Building a long-term brand to stand out in a short-term world*. McGraw Hill.

6. Patagonia (2024). 'Our core values'. *Patagonia*. Available at: https://www.patagonia.com/core-values/

Index

Note: *Italic* page number refer to *figures*